I0354477

CHASING KING'S KILLER

THE HUNT FOR MARTIN LUTHER KING, JR.'S ASSASSIN

JAMES L. SWANSON

SCHOLASTIC PRESS | NEW YORK

To my father, Lennart Swanson

(1930–2016)

And in memory of John Hope Franklin

(1915–2009)

FOREWORD
BY CONGRESSMAN JOHN LEWIS

I was fifteen years old—perhaps the same age as some of you—when I heard the voice of Martin Luther King, Jr. on the radio. I felt like he was speaking directly to me—like he was saying, "You, John Lewis, you, too, can do something!" But what could a young boy do to change the world?

Three years later, when I was eighteen, I wrote to Dr. King and told him I wanted to enroll at Troy State, a college that refused to admit African Americans. Dr. King invited me to come see him. I had no money, so he sent me a round-trip Greyhound bus ticket to Montgomery, Alabama. When we met he laughed and asked, "Who *is* this young man? Are *you* the boy from Troy?" We had a wonderful talk. He changed my life that day, and I joined the civil rights movement and committed myself to love, peace, and nonviolence.

The next years were a whirlwind: Sit-ins in 1960 at segregated lunch counters that refused to serve black people, where we were cursed, spit upon, had food and drinks poured over our heads, and were beaten; the Freedom Rides of 1961, where we rode interstate buses through the segregated South, and were attacked by mobs, and I was left beaten and unconscious, lying in a pool of blood. You might ask if I knew how dangerous it might be? Yes, I did. At dinner the night before our first trip, the Freedom Riders joked that this might be our "Last Supper." There was a real possibility that we might not return—that we might even be killed.

But somebody had to be willing to do *something*. And I knew this—the civil rights movement depended on young people. We had to take risks, to put ourselves in harm's way, so that others could stand up.

In 1963, during the March on Washington for Jobs and Freedom, I was asked—as chairman of the Student Nonviolent Coordinating Committee (SNCC)—to be one of the speakers. I was only twenty-three years old. There were 250,000 people spread out across the National Mall in front of the Lincoln Memorial when I saw Dr. King step up and say, "I have a dream."

In 1965, we marched from Selma to Montgomery, Alabama, to demonstrate for the Voting Rights Act. When our peaceful protest tried to cross the Edmund Pettus Bridge, the police attacked. I was hit with a nightstick and the blow fractured my skull. I thought I saw death, but I didn't die. I still have the scars on my head. For crossing a bridge. For standing up. For voting rights. For freedom.

Then came April 4, 1968, when an assassin's bullet changed the course of history. For those who lived through the death of Martin Luther King, Jr., something died in all of us that day. After the assassination, something died in America. The sense of hope, of optimism, of possibility was replaced by horror and despair. It was a dark, dark time. I never believed in any man as much as I believed in Martin Luther King, Jr. From the time I was fifteen until the day he died, he was the person who made me who I was. He made me the man I am. When Martin was killed I felt like I had lost part of myself. But we picked ourselves up yet again.

Then we suffered another loss. Just two months later, Senator Robert Kennedy was shot and killed. I was with him that night. I cried for all the fallen, all the countless individuals who gave everything they had, but I knew we couldn't stop. We couldn't give up. Sometimes we get bruised, sometimes we get knocked down, but we have the will, the courage, and the ability to get *up*. But there was one thing that didn't die—the dream.

In this thrilling, beautiful, and tragic book, James Swanson takes me back to the days of my youth, all the joys and all the sorrows. He portrays Dr. King as he really was: a man of bravery, vision, and hope. He captures the man I knew, my hero, my big brother, and my friend. It was fifty years ago, and I miss him still.

This is a book that every young American should read. James Swanson has told the story, and now I say to you: Tell the story, tell the story, and tell it over and over again.

JOHN LEWIS

Member of Congress
Washington, D.C.
September 21, 2017

TABLE OF
CONTENTS

A leader of his people tells
The Montgomery Story

STRIDE
TOWARD
FREEDOM

By
MARTIN
LUTHER
KING,
Jr.

Martin Luther King, Jr.'s first book, *Stride Toward Freedom*.

"A SNEEZE MEANT DEATH"

In the fall of 1958, Dr. Martin Luther King, Jr., a twenty-nine-year-old minister in Montgomery, Alabama, who had recently risen to national prominence as a civil rights activist, traveled to New York City to promote his first book.

He almost didn't make it out of town alive.

New York was his first stop on a national publicity tour for his book *Stride Toward Freedom.* The memoir was about his involvement in the Montgomery, Alabama, bus boycott. A local law had said that only whites were allowed to sit in the front of public buses; black passengers had to sit in back. The law also required that when a bus was full, blacks sitting in the back had to give up their seats to white people. To protest this racial discrimination, blacks refused to ride the buses of Montgomery.

King's leadership of the boycott had transformed him from a little-known preacher into an important civil rights leader. He was at the dawn of what promised to be a brilliant career.

Display ads featuring the book cover and King's photograph had already been placed in newspapers across the country. He was excited to travel to Manhattan, and he expected friendly treatment in the most important city in the North. Many New Yorkers were receptive to his message and hoped to see him in person. And King was eager to meet them.

King arrived in New York City on Monday, September 15, 1958. For several days, there would be book signings, media appearances, and public events. A highlight of the trip was a rally of five thousand people in front of the Hotel Theresa in Harlem on the evening of Friday, September 19. The baseball star Jackie Robinson appeared onstage; the famous musician Duke Ellington and his orchestra played; New York governor Averell Harriman and his opponent in the gubernatorial campaign, Nelson Rockefeller, made political speeches. And of course, King himself also spoke.

A group of twelve picketers struck a rare discordant note, some of them carrying signs that read BUY BLACK. They were led by Lewis Michaux, owner of the renowned National Memorial African Bookstore on West 125th Street, which specialized in black history, literature, and culture. And they were aggrieved that King was scheduled to sign books the next day at the white-owned Blumstein's department store just down the block. Although Michaux was hurt that he had not been asked to host this event, he and his followers staged a respectful demonstration.

Another unhappy person that night who was not so courteous was a strange, well-dressed black woman who stood behind the speaker's platform and heckled the white dignitaries as they addressed the crowd, yelling that she wanted nothing to do with anyone or anything white.

King ignored her.

"Many of you," he said, "had hoped I would come here to bring you a message of hate against the white man . . . I come here with no such message. Black supremacy is just as bad as white supremacy. I come here with a message of love rather than hate. Don't let any man make you stoop so low that you have hate. Have love in your hearts to those who would do you wrong."

These comments provoked the woman even more.

When the meeting was over, one of King's hosts worriedly suggested that he consider having a bodyguard the next day—his last in New York.

King dismissed the idea.

On Saturday, September 20, a little after 3:00 p.m., King arrived at Blumstein's department store, on West 125th Street between

Blumstein's department store on West 125th Street in New York City. On September 20, 1958, Martin Luther King, Jr., held a book signing here to promote his memoir, *Stride Toward Freedom*. It turned out to be a life-threatening event.

Seventh and Eighth Avenues. A desk and chair had been set up for him in a roped-off area behind the shoe department on the first floor. He sat down and posed for photographs with several dignitaries, including Arthur Spingarn, the legendary president of the NAACP, and Anna Arnold Hedgeman, a leader in the civil rights movement and assistant to New York City mayor Robert F. Wagner.

A stack of books awaited King's signature. He was not there to give a speech, but just to sit at the desk, chat one-on-one with customers, and autograph the books they bought. He enjoyed this kind of interaction: low-key, personal, and amiable.

King posed for more photographs, including one with an honor guard of young black girls who wore sashes over their right shoulders, emblazoned with the name of their school, Wadleigh Junior High. In the same photo, two smiling white boys stood in front of the desk, shaking hands with King, who beamed at them. It was a photograph that symbolized King's ideals of racial harmony.

King began to sign books, devoting a little time to each guest, exchanging friendly words. When the line had dwindled to about twenty people, a woman suddenly cut to the front. She was tall and dressed in an attractive jacket, white blouse, blue skirt, and heels. She wore earrings and fashionable cat-eye glasses, and she carried a big handbag. No one seemed to realize it was the angry woman from the previous night. Her name was Izola Ware Curry. She was forty-two and divorced, a Georgia native who had moved to New York and had worked as a maid.

The *Amsterdam News* published this photo of King shaking hands with children at his book signing at Blumstein's department store.

She paused in front of the desk. No one stood between her and King. She was much closer to him now than she'd been at the rally.

She faced King and looked into his eyes.

She possessed a loaded .32-caliber semiautomatic pistol that was concealed in her bra. She could have easily reached for it now, but she had another weapon hidden in her handbag, a Japanese letter opener in a bright crimson sheath. This was no ordinary letter opener: It was, according to someone who would soon have cause to examine it closely, an "extremely narrow, rigid, inflexible steel blade 6 to 8 inches in length, which had apparently been sharpened along its length to the point." With its wood handle, it resembled a minia-ture samurai sword and had the penetrating power of an ice pick.

"Are you Martin Luther King?" she asked.

"Yes, I am," King answered.

Curry shouted, "I've been after you for five years! You've made enough people suffer. I have to do it! I have to do it!"

For some reason, she had chosen the blade over the pistol, and grip-ping the letter opener in her hand, she thrust her arm up in the air.

Stunned onlookers—customers, schoolchildren, and others—were helpless to stop her as she swung her arm in a powerful, arcing blow.

King saw the blade bearing down on him and instinctively tried to parry it with his arm. His reaction deflected but did not block the blade's momentum. It sliced his hand, inflicting a flesh wound. Then Curry buried the letter opener in King's chest. It punched through his breastbone and lodged two and a quarter inches deep inside him. She had struck him so hard that the handle even broke off.

Anna Hedgeman, the mayor's assistant, was standing only a few feet away. "It happened so fast it was incredible," she said.

Photographer Vernoll Coleman was at Blumstein's doing public-ity work for King's publisher. "I was arranging a [photo] when the whole thing happened," he said. "I thought the woman had simply swung at him or slapped him. But when I took a second look I saw that thing sticking out of [his] chest."

Coleman reacted with a newsman's lightning instinct. He raised his Hasselblad camera and snapped a photograph that would appear

★★★★ FINAL

SUNDAY ⬤ NEWS

NEW YORK'S PICTURE NEWSPAPER ®

10¢

Vol. 38. No. 21   Copr. 1958 News Syndicate Co. Inc.   New York 17, N.Y., Sunday, September 21, 1958*   WEATHER: Rain, mild.

MARTIN LUTHER KING STABBED

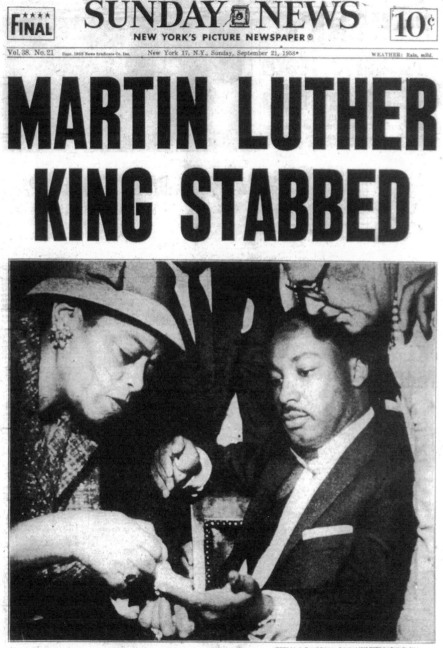

(NEWS foto by Vernoff Coleman; Copyright 1958 NEWS Syndicate Co. Inc.)

A Letter Opener in His Chest, the Rev. Martin Luther King has wounded hand treated by Nettie Carter Jackson, of Brooklyn, at W. 123d St. police station. Leader of bus boycott by Negroes in Montgomery, Ala., was stabbed by woman as he autographed copies of his book in Harlem store. —*Story on page 3*

The front page of a New York newspaper ran a photo of Martin Luther King, Jr., taken just after Izola Curry stabbed him. The letter opener is still in his chest, and a bystander is treating his cut hand.

in newspapers around the world: a dazed Martin Luther King, Jr., with a blade sticking out of his chest while a woman bent over him to wipe the blood from his wounded hand.

"Women began screaming," the photographer recalled, "and the crowd tried to get at this woman." One witness shouted, "She cut Dr. King!"

King hoped to calm them. "That's all right!" he said. "That's all right! Everything's going to be all right."

But he was in shock and he stayed seated. The dazed look on his face suggested that he did not fully comprehend what had just happened or how seriously he had been wounded. Blood oozed from the wound, staining his crisp white cotton dress shirt.

"I've been after him for years!" Curry screamed again. "I'm glad I done it!"

Then she tried to run away. The women in King's entourage chased her. Waving their umbrellas like clubs, they shouted: "Catch her, don't let her go!" Walter Pettiford, an advertising executive for the *Amsterdam News*, New York City's leading black newspaper, grabbed her by the left arm and spun her around. Harry Dixon, the store's floor manager, raised his hands and pleaded, "Please don't harm her."

Curry kept shouting: "Dr. King has ruined my life. He is no good . . . I've been after him for years. I finally was able to get him now."

A security guard named Clifford Jackson detained Curry, and he and a police officer hustled her out of the store and into a cab, bound for a nearby police station.

Izola Curry, in police custody, being escorted to the police station after stabbing Martin Luther King, Jr.

Someone approached King and reached for the letter opener, yielding to the irresistible temptation to yank the blade out, but a voice shouted: "Don't pull it out. You'll kill him." Removing the blade might allow blood to pour out of the wound like a cork being pulled out of a bottle.

No one on the scene knew it, but the blade was so close to King's aorta that any sudden expansion of his chest, from coughing or sneezing, could have pushed the main artery of the heart directly into the point of the blade. If that artery was punctured, King would bleed to death before he arrived at a hospital.

A dispatcher at Harlem Hospital received the first phone call. A voice on the other end said that there had been a stabbing at Blumstein's and asked for help. One minute later, an ambulance and its crew of driver Ronald Adams and nurse Russie Lee went racing down Seventh Avenue from the hospital to the department store. They did not know who had been attacked. Upon arriving and finding King with the blade in his chest, Lee ordered him not to stand up. Next she told Adams to bring the ambulance around to the back door of the store, on 124th Street. Then a police officer and Adams carried King, still sitting in the chair, to the ambulance, where Lee made sure that they laid their patient down gently on his back. Adams got behind the wheel, and the nurse climbed into the back to sit near King. "He was conscious, and I told him not to touch the letter opener," she recalled. "He didn't speak, but his eyes told me he knew what I meant."

A little after 4:00 p.m., almost a half hour after the attack, King, still conscious, was brought into the Harlem Hospital Emergency

Room. Doctors and nurses rushed to his side. Then he looked up and, startled, came face-to-face with a woman he recognized. It was Izola Curry! But she had not escaped from custody or tracked him to the hospital to kill him. Police officers had brought her there for King to identify her as his assailant.

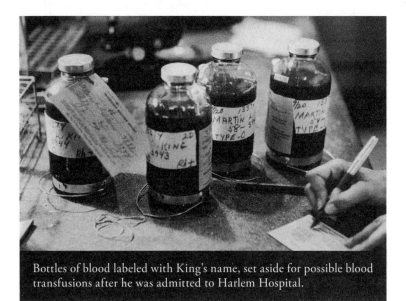

Bottles of blood labeled with King's name, set aside for possible blood transfusions after he was admitted to Harlem Hospital.

After this unnerving encounter, doctors decided that it was too risky to remove the weapon without surgery, so they hurriedly prepared King for the operation and placed him under anesthesia. He drifted off to sleep in the operating room, not knowing if he would reawaken.

But he did. A few hours later he opened his eyes.

He was still alive.

Word of the attack spread across the country. Black churches in New York City held prayer services. In Chicago, the legendary black newspaper the *Chicago Defender* reported that "the assault on King had barely been reported by radio newscasts when hundreds of telephone calls began to flood the switchboard." The calls "came from people who could not believe their ears, and from others who did believe the news, but wanted fuller details."

Police in New York told the press that Curry was "emotionally disturbed," but it was not long before someone raised the question of conspiracy. One newspaper reported: "One angle of the case now being studied by police as well as civil rights groups is the possibility that Mrs. Curry might have been 'put up' to an attempt to kill King by white segregation and White Citizens Council groups in the South."

Hinting that white racists might be behind the stabbing was dangerous talk. Speaking in Charlotte, North Carolina, the day after the attack, the famous evangelist preacher Reverend Billy Graham said that "blood would have run in the streets" if a white person had stabbed King. Graham concluded that a race war such as the country had never experienced would have broken out. He warned that racial tensions were at a breaking point, and that the help and understanding of people of all races was needed.

Once Izola Curry was in custody, every word she spoke to police officers or reporters confirmed the initial impression that she was mentally disturbed, rather than a conspirator. During her arraignment hearing in court the day after the stabbing, the magistrate observed her behavior and declared, "This woman is ill."

"I am not ill," Curry objected.

When the magistrate said, "I understand that this is the woman who is accused of stabbing the Reverend Dr. King with a knife," Curry corrected him and shouted, "No! It was a letter opener," as if that had made her attack any less dangerous.

From his hospital bed, King asked that this troubled woman not be punished. "I feel no ill-will toward [her] and know that thoughtful people will do all in their power to see that she gets the help she apparently needs." Charged with attempted murder, Curry was never put on trial. Instead, she was sent to a mental institution.

On October 3, King was released from Harlem Hospital and, after a month of rest and recuperation, made a full recovery. It seemed he was destined for more.

If Izola Curry had murdered Martin Luther King, Jr., on September 20, 1958, his assassination would have reshaped the arc of history and the destiny of twentieth-century America.

It is amazing how the actions of one anonymous person can change the future of not only a great person but an entire nation.

King's death would have created a void. Eloquent words would never have been spoken, great deeds would have gone undone, and grievous wrongs might not have been righted. Without Dr. King, the civil rights movement might have been thwarted, delayed, or gone in a different direction. Luck—destiny—God had spared him that day. He would live.

But the assassination attempt changed Martin Luther King, Jr. It reinforced in him a sense of fatalism, an acceptance of the dangers, risks, and uncertainty that he must make his peace with if he chose to continue to lead the civil rights movement. "The experience of these last few days has deepened my faith in the . . . spirit of nonviolence," he said. "I have now come to see more clearly [its] redemptive power."

A less courageous man might have been tempted to quit the movement and seek a safe and quiet life. But not King. As he said after the stabbing, "We must all be prepared to die." Strangely, King's surgical scars healed in the form of a cross over his heart. He joked that these were appropriate wounds for a minister of the gospel.

When Martin Luther King, Jr., arose from his hospital sickbed in the fall of 1958, he could not have imagined the future that awaited him. He was about to embark on an inspiring, decade-long journey that would lift him to the pinnacle of a symbolic mountaintop and make him one of the most pivotal leaders of the twentieth century. His greatest days lay ahead of him. He would become more than the champion of a great civil rights cause. For millions of people in the United States and around the world, he would become its beloved living, breathing symbol.

No, in September 1958, twenty-nine-year-old Dr. Martin Luther King, Jr., knew none of this . . .

Martin Luther King, Jr., and his wife, Coretta Scott King, on the steps of Harlem Hospital following his release after being stabbed by Izola Curry.

PART ONE

INTRODUCTION TO
MARTIN LUTHER KING, JR.,
AND THE CIVIL RIGHTS MOVEMENT

JIM CROW AMERICA

Martin Luther King, Jr., was born in Atlanta, Georgia, on January 15, 1929.

As he would learn, it was not easy to be black in early twentieth-century America. Even though the Civil War had ended in 1865, just sixty-four years before King's birth, African Americans still did not enjoy equal rights under the law. That war may have ended slavery, but generations later, black Americans were neither free nor equal citizens.

In the South, the states of the old Confederacy enacted so-called "Jim Crow" laws to strip black people of their civil rights. These unjust laws were based on the white supremacist belief that blacks were an inferior race. Racism was entrenched by the very institutions that were supposed to protect the rights of all citizens. Instead, these laws explicitly discriminated against blacks by creating "whites only" schools, theaters, hotels, restaurants, and other public accommodations. Blacks were not allowed to live in the same neighborhoods as whites, to attend state universities, or even to drink from the same water fountains. Throughout the South, signs reading WHITE and COLORED marked the boundaries of a segregated society.

Blacks were not allowed to exercise their political rights, either. Voter registration was suppressed, elections were rigged, and black candidates found it difficult to get on the ballot to run for office. They had little political power.

In the South, the state officials—the governors and mayors—were white, and so were the federal officeholders—the U.S. congressmen and senators.

The justice system was also unfair. In criminal trials, white judges and all-white juries often convicted—and even sentenced to death—black defendants on the flimsiest of evidence.

An African American man drinking at a segregated water cooler.

Through legal restrictions, whites controlled all aspects of blacks' lives: their rights, their movements in public, their activities, and their very bodies. This was accomplished not just through a system of racist laws and the power of the state. Intimidation, violence, and murder were essential tools in the suppression of African Americans. The Ku Klux Klan, a notorious racist terrorist organization whose symbol, a burning cross, subjected Southern blacks to horrific and senseless assaults. Local law enforcement—policemen and sheriffs—sometimes took part in these atrocious attacks, and some of them were even members of the Klan.

Between the late 1800s and the 1920s, over 3,200 black people had been lynched in America, mostly in the South. Sometimes white mobs broke into jails and hanged men who were awaiting trial. On other occasions, whites abducted blacks from the streets, the roads, or their own homes and hanged them for no reason at all, other than to create fear and reinforce white supremacy. There were even examples of lynch mobs degenerating into public celebrations, with photographers taking gruesome souvenir photos of victims that were later sold as postcards.

Racism was not only a Southern phenomenon. It existed in the North, too, where it was less blatant and obvious. And Northerners were not above racist violence. In 1908, rioting whites murdered blacks in Springfield, Illinois, Abraham Lincoln's hometown, and in Chicago in 1919.

Segregation also hurt blacks economically. Denied jobs, opportunities, and good wages because of their race, many blacks suffered in poverty and were not much better off than they had been during slavery. Without good schools or an education, there was no clear path to get ahead. Abraham Lincoln once compared slavery to a hopeless prison in which blacks were jailed behind a cell door locked with one hundred keys, making it impossible ever to escape. In the South, segregation and Jim Crow laws had kept African Americans in a similar prison ever since the Civil War.

This was the world into which Martin Luther King, Jr., was born. And the time had come for change.

Ku Klux Klan members with fiery crosses were a terrifying sight.

Martin Luther King, Jr., was the son of the prominent pastor of Atlanta's Ebenezer Baptist Church. During his earliest years, Martin's parents shielded him from the ugliest realities of racism.

Martin was raised as a member of the black elite. His family's status was based on their community service and religious leadership, not wealth. The King family was never poor, nor were they rich. Martin described his neighbors as people of average income. It was, he said, a "wholesome" community where crime was minimal and most people were deeply religious.

Martin joined the church when he was five. His father, grandfather, and great-grandfather were all preachers, and so was his uncle. Religion was a natural and important part of his life, and he attended church every Sunday.

He never suffered hunger or deprivation. "I have never experienced the feeling of not having the basic necessities of life. These things were always provided by my father, who always put his family first." Young Martin never had to drop out of school to work to earn money for the family. Looking back on his youth, he recalled: "The

Martin Luther King, Jr., with his family. Back row, from left to right: his mother, his father, and his maternal grandmother. Front row, his brother, his sister, and young Martin.

first twenty-five years of my life were very comfortable years. If I had a problem I could always call Daddy . . . Life had been wrapped up for me in a Christmas package."

Martin was a precocious child who possessed an inborn curiosity and a love of books and learning. One day his mother, Alberta, the daughter of a prominent minister, decided that Martin was old enough to hear what black parents today still call "The Talk": the conversation to prepare a black child for the racism he might encounter in the outside world. Martin never forgot it.

"My mother confronted the age-old problem of the Negro parent in America: how to explain discrimination and segregation to a small child . . . She told me about slavery, and how it ended with the Civil War. She tried to explain the divided system of the South— the segregated schools, restaurants, theaters, housing; the white and colored signs on drinking fountains, waiting rooms, lavatories— as a social condition rather than a natural order." Martin's mother said that she opposed these racist practices and told him that he must never allow them to make him feel inferior. "You are as good as anyone," she taught her firstborn son. But as much as his parents protected him from racism, he never forgot his early childhood encounters with segregation.

When Martin was six, a white boy who had been his playmate since they were three years old ended their friendship when he went to a white, segregated school. It crushed Martin, who admitted, "from that moment on I was determined to hate every white person." His parents admonished him that he should not hate.

Once when Martin's father took him to a shoe store, the salesman said that they would have to get up from their seats and move to the back of the store. His father, the elder Reverend King, got up and walked out: "We'll either buy shoes sitting here, or we won't buy shoes at all."

Martin suffered segregation at parks, swimming pools, schools, and movie theaters. One day when he was eight years old, his mother took him shopping in downtown Atlanta. A white woman slapped him in the face and spoke a vile insult: "You are that 'n∗∗∗∗∗' that stepped on my foot." That word, now considered so offensive that many books and newspapers will no longer print it, was once a common slur that whites used when speaking to or talking about blacks.

Martin remembered the time in high school when a white bus driver ordered him and a female teacher to give up their seats to white people—"it was the angriest I have ever been in my life"—and he remembered when a white policeman dared to call his father, one of the most distinguished men in Atlanta, "boy." It was a word meant to show disrespect to black men.

The summer before Martin started college, he went to Connecticut to work on a tobacco farm. The experience had a profound effect on him. He was treated as an equal of the young white local teens who worked with him in the fields. There were no WHITES ONLY signs on water fountains or soda machines. He could go to restaurants. And he could sit wherever he liked in theaters or buses or trains. He relished the temporary freedom from segregation that he enjoyed in the North. In sharp contrast, returning home to the Southern system depressed him. "I could never adjust to the separate waiting rooms, separate eating places, separate restrooms, partly because the separate was always unequal, and partly because the very idea of separation did something to my sense of dignity and self-respect."

In 1944, during the Second World War, Martin enrolled at the unusually young age of fifteen as a freshman at Morehouse College, a prominent black institution that both his father and his mother's father had attended. Martin already had a strong interest in racial and economic justice, but on campus he experienced an intellectual awakening when he read Henry David Thoreau's famous essay "Civil Disobedience." It was King's first exposure to the theory of nonviolent resistance. "Fascinated by the idea of refusing to cooperate with an evil system, I was so deeply moved that I reread the work several times. I became convinced that noncooperation with evil is as much a moral obligation as is cooperation with good."

In his senior year in college, before he had even graduated, Martin followed family tradition and was ordained at Ebenezer Baptist Church as a minister in February 1948. After graduating that June at age nineteen, he entered Crozer Theological Seminary in Pennsylvania for advanced religious training. In the spring of 1950, he experienced a second intellectual awakening when he traveled to Philadelphia to hear a sermon by Dr. Mordecai Johnson. Johnson was the president of Howard University, a famous black school in Washington, DC. The educator spoke about the leader of the Indian independence movement, Mohandas Gandhi. India had been a former colony of the British Empire, achieving independence only after the Second World War. Martin found Gandhi's philosophy of peaceful resistance to Great Britain's control over India "profound and electrifying."

In the fall of 1951, Martin entered Boston University's School of Theology to earn a doctorate degree. The next year he met a young woman named Coretta Scott. She had attended Antioch College in Ohio and was a student at the New England Conservatory of Music in Boston. A talented musician who wanted to be a concert singer, her physical beauty and intellectual nature proved impossible for Martin to resist. Martin and Coretta married in June 1953.

As a preacher's wife, Coretta was expected to support Martin's ministry and give up her dreams of travel and a glamorous career as a professional singer. Later in life, Martin acknowledged the sacrifices that "Corrie" had made. "She had to settle down to a few concerts here and there. Basically she has been a pastor's wife and mother of our four children." In September 1954, Martin became the pastor of the Dexter Avenue Baptist Church in Montgomery, Alabama. Nine months later, he received his PhD in theology and earned the right to be called doctor. After that, many of his closest associates would call him Doc. He joined the local branch of the NAACP (the National Association for the Advancement of Colored People). And in November 1955, his and Coretta's first child, a daughter, was born.

In the fall of 1955, Dr. Martin Luther King, Jr., was headed for a predictable, quiet life as a minister, husband, father, and respected local community leader. He seemed content to follow in his father's footsteps. He had no ambitions to become famous, to seek political office, or to become the leader of a national movement. If he

Martin Luther King, Jr., and his wife, Coretta, with daughter Yolanda and son Martin Luther King III.

had stayed on this path, it is possible that no one living outside Montgomery, Alabama, would have ever heard of Martin Luther King, Jr.

But before the end of the year, something happened that upended his life and set him on a new course.

MONTGOMERY BUS BOYCOTT

On December 1, 1955, a woman named Rosa Parks was arrested in Montgomery for violating the city's bus segregation law when she refused to give up her seat to a white passenger. Black leaders had been looking for an opportunity to challenge the law. A few days later, they elected Martin Luther King, Jr., as the head of the Montgomery Improvement Association (MIA). It was a new organization, and they wanted Martin to lead the campaign.

King and his colleagues decided that if blacks could not ride the buses of Montgomery as equal citizens, they would not ride them at all. To stay in business, the bus company depended on the fares paid by black passengers. If blacks boycotted the buses, the company's income would plummet. But African Americans needed the buses to get to and from work. So the MIA organized carpools. Many people walked. Some people even rode on horseback or in wagons or mule carts. And many white people volunteered to drive their maids, cooks, and nannies to work.

A policeman fingerprints Rosa Parks after she was arrested for violating the bus segregation law in Montgomery, Alabama.

It was not long before segregationists fought back with violence. On January 30, 1956, while Martin spoke at a meeting to support the bus boycott, his home was bombed. He was not there when it happened, but it was a frightening warning of what some whites were willing to do to resist civil rights. The bombing also made it clear that not only King but also his family were in danger.

The boycott lasted for about one year. It was a hardship, but it united the black community. On November 13, 1956, the Supreme Court of the United States ruled that the Montgomery, Alabama, bus segregation laws violated the Fourteenth Amendment of the United States Constitution's guarantee of equal treatment under the law.

The next month, the MIA voted to end the boycott. King was one of the first people to ride a desegregated bus, on which blacks

King rides on a desegregated bus following the Montgomery, Alabama, bus boycott and the Supreme Court ruling that bus segregation laws are unconstitutional.

would no longer have to sit in the back. In addition, no longer would they have to surrender their seats to white people. After everything that King and the movement had endured to fight for those rights, the day of victory was anticlimactic. The white bus driver wished King good morning, welcomed him aboard, and proceeded on his route as though nothing out of the ordinary had just happened.

But something extraordinary *had* happened to Martin Luther King, Jr. His leadership during the Montgomery bus boycott had made him famous. In May 1957, he was invited to speak in Washington, DC, at the Lincoln Memorial for an event called a Prayer Pilgrimage for Freedom.

King's portrait even appeared on the cover of *Time* magazine, a sign that the most influential news magazine in America had decided he was of national importance. It was an honor that few blacks had ever received.

And King had been elected president of the Southern Christian Leadership Conference. It was a new organization that would soon become one of the most important groups in the nation advocating for the civil rights of black Americans.

Martin Luther King, Jr., was a rising star. But then, on September 20, 1958, he was stabbed by Izola Curry. The injuries threatened to end King's life at the dawn of a brilliant career.

He had two choices—he could heed his close call with death, step out of the spotlight, and return to his quiet life. Or he could continue his work. He chose to recommit himself to the civil rights movement.

TWENTY CENTS

FEBRUARY 18, 1957

TIME

THE WEEKLY NEWSMAGAZINE

Montgomery, Alabama's
REV. MARTIN LUTHER KING

6.00 A YEAR

(REG. U.S. PAT. OFF.)

VOL. LXIX NO. 7

King appears on the cover of *Time*, one of the biggest news magazines of the era.

King realized that if he hoped to change history, he needed a grand strategy. It would not be enough to hold a few scattered and random boycotts and protests. King was realistic about what he was up against and the power of the system he opposed. In 1958, the civil rights movement faced a formidable task: overcoming the effects of a regime of slavery that had existed for two and a half centuries, from the early 1600s to 1865, the end of the Civil War. In addition, there was the unbearable injustice that had existed since 1865. The crushing oppression of 350 years could not be reversed overnight. It would take time. Great patience and many victories and setbacks would be required. It had taken a long time to abolish slavery. Similarly, King and the civil rights movement needed a long-term plan, a multipart strategy. But the regime King hoped to defeat would not surrender its power easily.

King's activism had propelled him to the forefront of the civil rights movement. He was the most eloquent of the leaders, so he became the spokesman and the symbol. But there were other important leaders, too. It was a cause and a movement that required more than one man to make it happen. King knew he needed help. So he formed a coalition of people and organizations. To win civil rights for black Americans, King pursued two goals simultaneously: He wanted to change the law, and he wanted to change public opinion.

In the first prong of this one-two punch, King decided that peaceful, nonviolent but relentless public protests, demonstrations, marches, and speeches could call attention to civil rights violations. He believed that publicity, especially newspaper and television coverage, could shame the opponents of civil rights. And it could win over people of goodwill—including whites—to the cause. King's paramount tactic was to influence blacks to resist injustice with nonviolence.

As he led this moral crusade for equal rights for all African Americans, King also emphasized the religious and moral dimension of the cause. Christian ministers, churches, and religious faith played a big role in the fight for civil rights. King often said that he was a Christian minister first and a civil rights leader second.

The second prong of the strategy was to use the law. Civil rights lawyers continued to go to court and challenge unjust and unconstitutional laws, as they had done when they overturned school segregation in the famous case of *Brown v. Board of Education* in 1954. The civil rights movement sought to repeal laws that discriminated against blacks at schools and in public accommodations like restaurants, hotels, and other places. But King wanted to do more than just overturn bad laws. He wanted the United States Congress to pass new laws to protect the right of blacks to vote, and to have equal access to housing and employment.

King knew he needed to do more than change the law. He needed to change human hearts and minds, too. Racist attitudes had been woven into the fabric of American life for centuries. It was a daunting and gigantic task. Was King was up to the challenge?

ON THE RISE: LUNCH COUNTERS, FREEDOM RIDERS, AND OLE MISS

In February 1959, Martin traveled to India. He met spiritual leaders and learned more about Mohandas Gandhi's beliefs in pacifism and the techniques of nonviolent protest, which had been used to win independence for India from its colonial ruler, Great Britain. King's trip to India influenced the mission he was about to undertake.

On February 1, 1960, the civil rights "sit-in" movement officially began when four black students asked for service at a "whites only" Woolworth lunch counter in Greensboro, North Carolina. When they were not served, the students refused to leave. This method of nonviolent protest spread quickly to other parts of the South. As these sit-ins grew in numbers, enraged whites humiliated them by shouting racist curses and dumping food and beverages on their heads. On October 19, during a sit-in in Atlanta, Martin and fifty other protesters were arrested.

The Woolworth lunch counter in Greensboro, North Carolina.

The authorities wanted to teach King a lesson, so, to frighten him, the police jailed him for a prior minor traffic violation. Alone, isolated from his family and friends, he was in danger of harm at the hands of white policemen. On October 26, toward the end of the presidential election campaign, one of the candidates, John F. Kennedy, helped free King from jail. Less than two weeks later, on November 8, 1960, Kennedy won the presidential election by little more than 100,000 votes. Many people believed that his concern for Dr. King helped win votes for his narrow victory.

The next year, in May 1961, the first Freedom Riders boarded two interstate buses in Washington, DC, bound for New Orleans, Louisiana, 1,100 miles away. These initial thirteen riders were a group of seven black and six white pacifists intending to challenge the segregation laws in Southern bus stations and on the buses

A Freedom Riders bus burns after it is attacked.

themselves. White racists met them with violence. Just south of Anniston, Alabama, their bus was burned, and in Birmingham, Alabama, they were beaten by mobs. These attacks revealed the culture of rising violence that Martin Luther King, Jr., faced.

Another group of Freedom Riders that traveled from Nashville, Tennessee, was beaten in Montgomery, Alabama. To protect the riders from further attacks, National Guard soldiers escorted them as far as Jackson, Mississippi. But when they got there, they were attacked, arrested, and jailed.

That fall in November and December 1961, Albany, Georgia, became the focus of new challenges to unfair racial laws. Freedom Riders rode buses and trains to the town and were arrested. In later demonstrations, Dr. King and more than five hundred protesters

Freedom Riders John Lewis and James Zwerg, beaten and bloodied, after an attack.

were also arrested and sent to jail. But protests for equal rights in Albany proved futile because clever local officials avoided violent, public confrontations with the civil rights activists. King considered his efforts there a failure.

In 1962, the movement won a victory when, on October 1, James Meredith became the first black student to enroll at the University of Mississippi—"Ole Miss." His presence on campus caused student rioting because whites did not want to allow blacks to attend college with them. Federal troops had to be sent to the university to protect Meredith and escort him to class. But behind each victory, there remained the threat of violence.

TRAGEDIES AND TRIUMPHS: PROTESTS IN BIRMINGHAM, A LETTER FROM JAIL, AND A MARCH ON WASHINGTON

The year 1963 would prove to be one of the most dramatic and event-packed years of the twentieth century. It would see Martin Luther King's greatest triumph, and also great tragedies.

On April 12, 1963, Martin protested the segregation of eating facilities in Birmingham, Alabama. After sit-in demonstrations, King was arrested. While in solitary confinement, he wrote what would become one of his most famous statements about civil rights—the "Letter from Birmingham Jail." It was a response to his critics among the white clergy who claimed that resisting injustice was "unwise and untimely." King disagreed: "Injustice must be exposed, with all the tension its exposure creates, to the light of human conscience and the air of national opinion before it can be cured." And he concluded, "Oppressed people cannot remain oppressed forever."

Nonviolent demonstrations in Birmingham continued the next

Martin Luther King, Jr., sits behind bars in the Jefferson County Courthouse in Birmingham, Alabama.

month. On May 2, almost one thousand black children, from grade school through high school, marched in the streets, singing "We Shall Overcome." They, too, were arrested and taken to jail. The following day, students kept marching. Eugene "Bull" Connor, the Birmingham Commissioner of Public Safety, ordered the police to use dogs and fire hoses to subdue the protesters. News photos of dogs attacking black children and powerful jets of water knocking them off their feet were published around the world, provoking international outrage against the treatment of blacks, and winning sympathy for the civil rights movement.

Police dogs attack civil rights demonstrators

A powerful water spray from a fire hose envelops protesters.

Americans—including President Kennedy—watched it all on television. Ugly images of racist mobs exposed the evil of racial discrimination in "the land of the free." On June 11, 1963, Kennedy decided he could wait no more and gave a televised address to the nation about civil rights:

"One hundred years of delay have passed since President Lincoln freed the slaves, yet their heirs, their grandsons, are not fully free. They are not yet freed from the bonds of injustice. They are not yet freed from social and economic oppression. And this Nation, for all its hopes and all its boasts, will not be fully free until all its citizens are free."

And he concluded:

> "The heart of the question is whether all Americans are to
> be afforded equal rights and equal opportunities, whether
> we are going to treat our fellow Americans as we want to
> be treated. If an American, because his skin is dark, can-
> not eat lunch in a restaurant open to the public, if he
> cannot send his children to the best public school avail-
> able, if he cannot vote for the public officials who will
> represent him, if, in short, he cannot enjoy the full and
> free life which all of us want, then who among us would
> be content to have the color of his skin changed and stand
> in his place? Who among us would then be content with
> the counsels of patience and delay?"

Racists who supported segregation and opposed civil rights did
not care what President Kennedy said—they were not going to go
down without a fight. The very next day, June 12, Medgar Evers, the
leader of the NAACP in Mississippi, was gunned down outside his
home in Jackson by a white supremacist.

To give momentum to their cause, civil rights leaders decided to
hold a huge public rally in the nation's capital that summer: They
called it the March on Washington for Jobs and Freedom. On
August 28, 1963, more than 250,000 people from all over America
gathered on the National Mall to support civil rights.

With the Lincoln Memorial as a backdrop, leaders of religious,

Martin Luther King, Jr., walks with demonstrators during the March on Washington for Jobs and Freedom.

labor, and political organizations gave short speeches. Dr. Martin Luther King, Jr., was the last scheduled speaker.

King began reading from his prepared text:

> "But one hundred years later, the Negro still is not free; one hundred years later, the life of the Negro is still crippled by the manacles of segregation and the chains of discrimination; one hundred years later, the Negro lives on a lonely island of poverty in the midst of a vast ocean of material prosperity; one hundred years later, the Negro is

The sculpture of Abraham Lincoln looks over Martin Luther King, Jr., as he addresses the crowd at the March on Washington.

still languished in the corners of American society and finds himself in exile in his own land."

But as King spoke, he sounded flat and seemed to lose his place. His speech was not rousing the crowd. King was an experienced and effective speaker, but he had never addressed such a huge audience. The great gospel singer Mahalia Jackson was seated near where he stood at the podium.

She called out to him: "Tell them about the dream, Martin!"

Inspired by Mahalia, King ended the rally with the words of the glorious "I Have a Dream" speech. He began:

"I say to you today, my friends, so even though we face the difficulties of today and tomorrow, I still have a dream."

Repeating over and over the line "I have a dream," King told his audience that he believed one day racial oppression would be overcome and that all Americans would "one day live in a nation where they will not be judged by the color of their skin but by the content of their character."

It was a personal triumph—the most glorious moment in King's life up until then. In just five years, he had experienced a meteoric rise. In 1958, he had survived a near-fatal stabbing. Now, in 1963, his Lincoln Memorial speech had transformed him into one of the most famous and admired men in the world. The March on Washington created a wildly optimistic mood for the civil rights movement that promised to redeem 1963 from the bad things that had happened earlier that year. President Kennedy invited King and the other organizers of the march to the White House. Anything seemed possible now. At that moment, it seemed like 1963 would turn out to be a very good year after all.

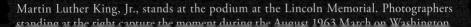

Martin Luther King, Jr., stands at the podium at the Lincoln Memorial. Photographers standing at the right capture the moment during the August 1963 March on Washington.

DISASTER AND HOPE: A BOMBING IN BIRMINGHAM, THE ASSASSINATION OF A PRESIDENT, AND A NEW LEADER

Only a month later, the year 1963 took a disastrous turn. On September 15, the Sixteenth Street Baptist Church in Birmingham, Alabama, was bombed when Ku Klux Klansmen planted dynamite next to the church. When the bomb exploded, four little girls attending Sunday school were killed. Many others were injured. It earned the city the nickname "Bombingham." King was devastated.

"These children," he said in his eulogy for the girls:

"unoffending; innocent and beautiful—were victims of one of the most vicious and tragic crimes ever perpetrated against humanity. . . . So . . . in spite of the darkness of

The four young girls killed in the bombing (from left to right).
Top: Denise McNair, Carole Robertson; Bottom: Addie Mae Collins, Cynthia Wesley.

this hour we must not despair. We must not become bitter; nor must we harbor the desire to retaliate with violence. No, we must not lose faith with our white brothers."

And as he concluded his sermon, King uttered a heartbreaking farewell: "Good night, sweet princesses, may the flight of angels take thee to thy eternal rest." It was from Shakespeare's *Hamlet*, when Horatio said, "Good night, sweet prince—and flights of angels sing thee to thy rest."

The killings, as horrible as they were, changed many people's attitudes and created more widespread sympathy for the civil rights movement.

After those depraved child murders in Birmingham, it seemed that 1963 could not possibly get worse. But it did. On November 22, 1963, a week before Thanksgiving, President John F. Kennedy was assassinated during a visit to Dallas, Texas. His murder stunned the nation. King feared that the tragedy foreshadowed his own fate. As he and Corrie watched Kennedy's funeral on television, he told his wife, "This is what is going to happen to me."

Upon the assassination of John F. Kennedy, the vice president, Lyndon Baines Johnson, was sworn in as the new leader of the country. There were many questions. Who was this new man? Some blacks feared the worst about this Southerner from Texas. What were his views on blacks? On civil rights?

Johnson had given a clue earlier that year, at the battlefield of Gettysburg, on Memorial Day 1963. One hundred years after the

Lyndon B. Johnson is sworn in as president on board Air Force One, following John F. Kennedy's assassination.

bloodiest battle of the Civil War, Johnson had delivered a speech as brief as Abraham Lincoln's Gettysburg Address, and in many ways as powerful. Johnson said that a century after slavery, blacks were not really free:

> "One hundred years ago, the slave was freed . . . One hundred years later, the Negro remains in bondage to the color of his skin."

Johnson argued that the fate of America depended on ensuring equal rights for all its citizens:

> "In this hour, it is not our respective races which are at stake—it is our nation. Let those who care for their country come forward, North and South, white and Negro, to lead the way . . . The Negro says, 'Now.' Others say, 'Never.' The voice of responsible Americans—the voice of those who died here and the great man who spoke here—their voices say, 'Together.' There is no other way . . . Until justice is blind to color, until education is unaware of race, until opportunity is unconcerned with the color of men's skins, emancipation will be a proclamation but not a fact. To the extent that the proclamation of emancipation is not fulfilled in fact, to that extent we shall have fallen short of assuring freedom to the free."

King's relationship with JFK had been complicated and sometimes difficult. Kennedy had been a reluctant civil rights warrior. Yes, he had given speeches and hosted civil rights leaders at the White House. But he was distant. His brother, Attorney General Robert F. Kennedy, had worried that embracing King too eagerly might hurt Kennedy's chances for reelection in 1964. RFK was suspicious of King. He feared King was anti-American and had secret ties to communism.

In Lyndon Johnson, Martin Luther King, Jr., had found, at last, his great political partner. LBJ proved to be an enthusiastic supporter of civil rights. Once out from under Kennedy's shadow, the real Johnson emerged. In a speech to a joint session of Congress four days after the president's assassination, Johnson called for the earliest possible passage of a civil rights bill. He was determined to pass the bill within one year, sometime in 1964.

FROM THE CIVIL RIGHTS BILL AND THE NOBEL PRIZE TO A MURDER AND A SLANDER

Over the next whirlwind year, the president and the preacher joined forces to create landmark legislation, the Civil Rights Act, which was signed into law on July 2, 1964. This act prohibited racial discrimination in public accommodations, employment, and voting. The law carried on Lincoln's legacy and, though it had taken a century to do so, it completed some of the unfinished work of the Civil War. It was a historic occasion, and President Johnson invited Martin Luther King and other civil rights leaders to the White House to witness his signing the act into law.

However, Johnson and King did not rest upon their laurels—they actively set out to pass more civil rights legislation. Segregationists quickly responded with violence. On August 4, the bodies of three murdered civil rights workers—James Chaney (black), Michael

King meets with President Lyndon B. Johnson in the Oval Office at the White House a few weeks after the November 1963 assassination of President Kennedy.

Schwerner (white), and Andrew Goodman (white)—were recovered near Philadelphia, Mississippi. These were some of the most notorious killings of the civil rights movement.

After this terrible event, King received uplifting news that fall.

On October 14, it was announced that King would be awarded the Nobel Peace Prize for his work in advancing civil rights through nonviolent methods. This immense honor, however, was condemned at a press conference by J. Edgar Hoover, the director of the FBI, who shockingly called King "the most notorious liar in the country." The FBI had been investigating King for several years, and Hoover had developed an increasingly negative view of him.

He had two major motives for disliking King. First, as head of the FBI, Hoover was a "law and order" advocate. He was irritated by and hated challenges to legal authority, and he believed that King's tactics—massive marches and civil disobedience—broke the law. Second, he suspected that King had come under the sway of powerful communist influences both in the United States and in the Soviet Union at the height of the Cold War.

After Hoover's press conference, he wrote a secret letter to the FBI's head of domestic intelligence, William Sullivan, stating that King's "exposure is long overdue" and he was about to get what he deserved.

Hoover's letter prompted Sullivan to craft his own letter: an anonymous, threatening missive to King. This letter pretended to be from a civil rights supporter who was angry with King and wanted to chastise him for his alleged moral failings. Sullivan mailed the note about one month before the Nobel Prize award ceremony in early December 1964. The package also contained FBI audiotape recordings of King's phone calls and meetings. Sullivan threatened to expose King unless he did a truly shocking thing: kill himself before he received the prize. It gave him a deadline, demanding that he commit suicide within the next thirty-four days or the anonymous sender would expose King the day he was to be awarded the Nobel Peace Prize.

King knew exactly who had sent him the letter and the audio recordings of FBI wiretaps that accompanied it. Hoover and Sullivan could not have seriously believed they could force King to take his own life. But they wanted to harass him and let him know that he was under constant FBI surveillance. Indeed, the agency had even

JOHN EDGAR HOOVER
DIRECTOR

Federal Bureau of Investigation
United States Department of Justice
Washington, D. C.

November 19, 1964

PERSONAL

Dear Bill:

I want to tell you how much I appreciate your note of today concerning the press conference which I had yesterday with the Washington women reporters. I have always been reluctant about holding press conferences and have only held one or two in the period during which I have been Director. However, these women reporters have been most persistent to have a briefing on the work of the Bureau and there were a number of things that I wanted to also get off my chest at the same time, so I took the occasion to see the group yesterday. I not only briefed them upon the structure of the Bureau and its accomplishments, but also dealt with some of the recent criticism which has been made of me personally and of the Bureau. I had no expectation that it would stir up as much publicity as it has. I realized, of course, that there would be articles in the various papers in the country, but I have been flooded today with telegrams from all sections of the country and out of the many hundreds that have been received, there have only been two or three which have criticized me for what I had to say about Martin Luther King. I share your view in thinking that his exposure is long overdue and maybe he is now beginning to get his just deserts. I certainly hope so.

It is grand to know that I have the support and goodwill of my close associates in the Bureau.

Sincerely,

[signature]

Mr. William C. Sullivan
Federal Bureau of Investigation
Washington, D. C.

J. Edgar Hoover's secret letter, warning that King's "exposure is long overdue" and that "he is now beginning to get his just deserts." It is published here for the first time.

penetrated King's circle—one of his associates was actually a paid FBI spy and informant.

King ignored the intimidation and traveled to Oslo, Norway, where he was awarded the Nobel Peace Prize on December 10, 1964. At age thirty-five, he was the youngest person in history to receive it. This prestigious honor brought worldwide attention to him and the civil rights movement.

NEW CHALLENGES AND WARNING SIGNS: THE ASSASSINATION OF MALCOLM X, THE BATTLE FOR SELMA, THE VOTING RIGHTS ACT, AND THE WATTS RIOTS

By the mid-1960s, a climate of racial and political violence had become part and parcel of American public life. White segregationists continued to resist the progress of the civil rights movement with intimidation and violence. At the same time, the assassination of President Kennedy had caused many people to lose confidence in our government and institutions.

A Nation of Islam minister and civil rights leader named Malcolm X was impatient with Martin Luther King's strategy of nonviolence. He thought it was too passive a tactic and that it would

Martin Luther King, Jr., and Malcolm X shake hands after the first and only time they met, on March 26, 1964.

take too long for blacks to obtain equal rights. He also disagreed with King's goal of full integration into white society. Instead, Malcolm X advocated that blacks adopt more aggressive tactics to defend themselves, and that, in their quest for civil rights, they should not seek integration. He thought that mixing with white society was poisonous and dangerous for blacks.

Like Martin Luther King, Jr., Malcolm X was a charismatic leader and a brilliant speaker. But they were different leaders on different paths. Despite their fame, they met only once.

On February 21, 1965, Malcolm X was assassinated in the Audubon Ballroom, in New York City, while beginning to give a speech to the Organization of Afro-American Unity. Three black men in the audience—followers of a rival leader in the Nation of Islam movement—stood up and shot him. Although Malcolm X had not been murdered by a white man, the assassination furthered the idea that people who had political disagreements were now more likely to settle their disputes with violence—even murder. The death of Malcolm X was an ill omen that foreshadowed an emerging truth: It was dangerous to be a black leader in America.

Two weeks later, with the shadow of murder still in the air, Martin Luther King, Jr., led the civil rights movement back to Alabama to urge Congress to support the federal Voting Rights Act. Several million blacks in the South had been disenfranchised by statewide efforts to deprive them of the right to vote. A man named Jimmie Lee Jackson had recently been killed while supporting voter registration in Selma, Alabama. King's Southern Christian Leadership

Conference, along with several other groups, organized a protest for March 7.

Civil rights supporters planned to walk the fifty miles between Selma and Montgomery, the state capital. They were stopped at the Edmund Pettus Bridge, where state troopers attacked the marchers with clubs and tear gas. The event became known as Bloody Sunday. The violence and tragedy did not end there: Two days later, whites beat to death a white minister, James Reeb, who had come to Alabama to support voting rights.

On March 21, under protection from National Guard troops, the march from Selma to Montgomery began again. This time it crossed

John Lewis being beaten by police in Selma.

the Pettus Bridge. On March 25, near the state capitol building in Montgomery, King addressed a rally of more than fifty thousand people. He gave an inspiring and defiant speech and vowed that he and the civil rights movement would never give up, repeating the positive encouragement:

> "We are on the move now. The burning of our churches will not deter us. We are on the move now. The bombing of our homes will not dissuade us. We are on the move now. The beating and killing of our clergymen and our young people will not divert us. We are on the move now."

King continued, "Like an idea whose time has come, not even the marching of mighty armies can halt us." King called for action: a march to the American dream, and a march on segregated housing, segregated schools, poverty, ballot boxes. However, he acknowledged that progress would not be fast or easy.

> "I know you are asking today, 'how long will it take?'
> "How long? Not long, because 'no lie can live forever.'
> "How long? Not long, because 'you shall reap what you sow.'
> "How long? Not long, because the arc of the moral universe is long, but it bends toward justice."

His words gave courage to his listeners, but the day's success, as with so many other moments of triumph, was marred by violence. That night a white civil rights volunteer from Michigan was murdered along Route 80, the scene of the march.

There was a moment of light, however, when on August 6, the Voting Rights Act of 1965 became law. This legislation followed up the Civil Rights Act of 1964 and gave additional protections to the political rights of blacks and guaranteed the right to register to vote and cast a ballot. But by now, many black communities had become frustrated by the oppression of their rights. On August 11, 1965, these feelings triggered a five-day riot in Watts, a predominantly black section of Los Angeles, which left thirty-four dead. Such events did not presage an auspicious year in 1966.

A YEAR OF DOUBTS AND DIVISIONS: CHICAGO, BLACK PANTHERS, AND MILITANTS

In January 1966, King tried to take the civil rights movement north to Chicago to campaign for improvements in housing and schools. Although the city was not in the South, Chicago was one of the most segregated cities in America. Blacks and whites did not live in the same neighborhoods. Many blacks lived in poor communities on the city's South and West Sides, so they rarely socialized, and their children did not attend the same schools. Mayor Richard Daley, one of the most powerful political bosses in America, kept the peace by awarding loyal black subordinates with power and influence in their own neighborhoods, called wards.

That summer in 1966, King lived temporarily in Chicago in his attempt to organize a civil rights movement there. It was hard and dangerous work. When he led a march through a segregated neighborhood, he was stoned by angry "white power" mobs. King said he had never seen such vicious hatred, not even in the Deep South. Many did not support him, including local black leaders who viewed King as an outside agitator ignorant of their ways, and some of those leaders even sided with Mayor Daley against him.

It was a major setback, and King's failure in Chicago shocked and depressed him. It made him wonder if his work made any difference, especially as rival civil rights leaders rejected his strategy of nonviolence and sought greater influence over the direction of the movement.

Dr. King's doubts stemmed from the fact that the civil rights movement was changing by the mid-1960s. The movement had never been monolithic, and King had never been its only voice. Other leaders like Malcolm X had emerged, and many had become frustrated with King's strategy of nonviolence and the religious practice of turning the other cheek. Some of them even began speaking of Dr. King with disrespect, mocking him as "De Lawd" (The Lord).

By this time, King was almost forty years old. The young and upcoming generation of activists—some in their late teens or early twenties—thought his approach was too conservative. They thought and even dressed differently from King: he in a dark suit and tie, they in less formal clothing. Impatient, their voices called for a more radical response to white racism and violence. They argued that the civil rights movement had become too passive, and too accommodating to white opinion. They saw nonviolence as a kind of appeasement or surrender, and advocated that white violence be met with self-defense. They wanted to fight back.

A line of Black Panther Party members.

Several major developments occurred in the summer and fall of 1966. In June, Stokely Carmichael, the new chairman of the Student Nonviolent Coordinating Committee (SNCC), shouted the slogan "Black Power" in public for the first time. A few months later, in October, the Black Panther Party for Self-Defense was formed by Huey Newton and Bobby Seale in Oakland, California. Carmichael, Newton, and Seale rejected King's philosophy of peaceful resistance and nonviolence. They said it made blacks the victims of violent racists. Too many innocent lives had been lost to murder, while thousands of other blacks had been beaten or abused, sometimes the victims of police brutality. It was time, they argued, for blacks to fight back and defend themselves.

For King, this was an especially difficult time, as—during the same period—J. Edgar Hoover's FBI kept him under surveillance, violated his privacy, and tried to destroy his personal life.

Martin Luther King, Jr., remained a great leader and public speaker, but he began privately to experience self-doubt. The responsibility of leading a historic movement for more than a decade was a crushing burden.

Was it all too much, he asked himself, *for one man to bear?*

King sits with civil rights leader Andrew Young in an airport. King spent a great deal of time away from home, traveling on behalf of the movement.

SPLITTING THE MOVEMENT AND OPPOSITION TO THE VIETNAM WAR

In 1967, Martin Luther King, Jr., split the civil rights movement. The division was caused not by something at home in America, but by a war halfway around the world in Vietnam. King himself set the tone for the year with the publication of his latest book, aptly titled in the form of a question: *Where Do We Go from Here?: Chaos or Community.*

The United States government intervened in the conflict to stop communism from spreading throughout Vietnam and into the rest of Southeast Asia. America supported the government of South Vietnam against the communist threat, while the other side was fighting to unify both North and South Vietnam under a communist government.

American involvement in the conflict quickly escalated. By 1963, President Kennedy had sent almost twenty thousand troops to Vietnam, and by 1967, President Johnson had sent several hundred

The war in Vietnam became one of the most controversial and divisive military conflicts in American history. Dr. King emerged as one of the most outspoken opponents of the war.

thousand. However, victory over communist forces still seemed out of reach. The war dragged on endlessly, and more Americans were dying in Vietnam every day. By the end of March 1967, more than ten thousand American soldiers had been killed in Vietnam. Importantly, many of them were black and had been drafted and sent to fight against their will.

The war in Vietnam deeply troubled King. On April 4, 1967, he gave one of the most important speeches of his life, setting out his opposition to it. Speaking at the famous Riverside Church in New York City, King said it was time for the civil rights movement to expand its traditional goals and tactics—using the courts to overturn racist laws; staging sit-ins, public protests, and big marches to fight racial segregation; and passing new laws to guarantee civil and equal rights. King wanted to do more than help African Americans. He called for a new campaign to fight for social justice for people of all races, for economic equality, and for world peace. And he demanded that the United States end the war in Vietnam.

It was risky for King to link his opposition to the Vietnam War to the civil rights movement. In fact, his antiwar stance divided the movement. Many black leaders and rank-and-file supporters criticized him. Shouldn't he, they asked, continue to devote his time and energy to the cause of civil rights at home rather than to a foreign conflict? The journey from slavery to freedom was not over, and there were still important battles to be fought and won. Why did he want to distract the movement now at this crucial moment and divert his efforts to a new cause? Many black leaders worried that King was taking the spotlight off their core mission: civil rights for African Americans.

King's antiwar speech was a direct attack on a major foreign policy of the United States. Young American soldiers were fighting and dying in the jungles of Southeast Asia. To many of his critics, his antiwar stance looked unpatriotic. Such a stance risked alienating several groups: the white Americans who had supported the goals of the civil rights movement; his political supporters and allies in Congress, those senators and representatives who supported legislation like the Civil Rights Act of 1964 and the Voting Rights Act of 1965; and his core group, black Americans.

Worst of all, King's vocal opposition to the war infuriated the president of the United States. This was not just any president— this was the larger-than-life Lyndon Baines Johnson, the white

Southerner from Texas who had risked his political future when he sided with King and the cause of equal civil rights for African Americans. Johnson had been King's ally, and the president treated his antiwar stance as a personal betrayal. Martin Luther King, Jr., had not only alienated the most powerful man in the world, but he had also turned his friend and partner against him.

The response nationwide was anger, as many black leaders criticized King harshly, more than they had ever dared to before. All the major newspapers and magazines condemned him. But King refused to back down. On April 15, 1967, he gave a speech in New York City in front of the United Nations: "To return to the road of peace, we should take the initiative in bringing a halt to this tragic war," he said. "We must all speak out in a multitude of voices against this most cruel and senseless war. The thunder of our voices will be the only sound stronger than the blast of bombs and the clamor of war hysteria."

King's words mattered and began to change the tone of the debate. He spoke later that month at the University of Minnesota, where he said the Vietnam War had "divided our country [and] invited hatred, bigotry, and violence." He argued that it was not his opposition to the war that had distracted the movement from civil rights, but that it was the war that had "diverted attention from civil rights." The reaction was surprisingly positive, and some students even carried signs saying that King should run for president of the United States in 1968.

On April 23, 1967, King gave a press conference in Cambridge, Massachusetts, home to Harvard University. "It is time now," he said, "to meet the escalation of the war in Vietnam with an escalation of opposition. There can be no freedom without peace and no peace without justice."

Martin Luther King was on dangerous ground. His antiwar stance threatened to ruin his reputation and credibility as a leader, and to undermine the progress of the whole civil rights movement.

PART TWO
COLLISON COURSE

A JAIL BREAK

In April 1967, two things happened that would change the destiny of the nation, and of Dr. King. He set the first one in motion himself with his opposition to the Vietnam War, but he had no control over—and was not even aware of—the second. On the same day Martin Luther King, Jr., gave his press conference in Cambridge, Massachusetts, to oppose the Vietnam War, something happened a thousand miles away. Something no one could have imagined would have any significance whatsoever to the life or work of Dr. King.

That day, a convicted felon escaped from the Missouri State Penitentiary in Jefferson City. He had tried but failed to escape several times before. This time he succeeded.

The inmate came to breakfast on the Sunday morning of April 23, 1967. He worked in the prison kitchen, so he had all the supplies he needed for his journey.

"I brought with me in a sack of twenty candy bars, a comb, a razor and blades, a piece of mirror, soap, and a transistor radio . . . I ate a good breakfast of about six eggs since I knew this might be my last meal for a while."

Then the inmate changed clothes. He had to. In the outside world, his prison uniform would have marked him instantly as an escaped convict and might lead to his quick arrest.

"I went to the bread room where I had hidden a white shirt and a pair of standard green prison pants that I had dyed black with stencil ink." That outfit would allow him to pass as a civilian. He dressed in the white shirt and black pants, and then he put on his jail clothes over them. He transferred the contents of his sack into his pockets and stuffed the empty bag under his shirts. He hid in his shoes three hundred dollars that he had made from black-market trading.

Then he entered the kitchen bakery, which supplied bread not only to the inmates behind the walls but also to prisoners who worked nearby on several farms. Workers had just piled loaves of fresh, warm bread into boxes measuring about four feet by three feet by three feet. The boxes were ready to load onto trucks that drove the bread to the farms. His accomplices, two or three other convicts who had agreed to assist his escape, helped him step into a breadbox. It was just big enough to conceal a crouching man hiding on top of the squashed loaves of bread. Then, his accomplices lifted the box and stacked it in a truck on top of the other containers. When the truck drove through a tunnel leading out of the prison, guards failed to search the breadboxes—and the convict rode to freedom, right through the open gates! When the vehicle stopped on a street near the Missouri River Bridge, the stowaway lifted the lid, and he jumped out of the truck. He was lucky: The driver did not even see him as he scrambled away.

"I ran to the railroad tracks and along the river until I was sure nobody could see me. Then I took off my prison clothes." He discarded the black pants but kept the shirt to wear at night when it was cold. He hid under a railroad bridge during daylight and listened to the radio, but he heard no news about his escape. He walked all night, stopping only to eat some of his candy bars.

On the second day, he hid again during daylight and listened to the radio. His escape had still not been reported on the news. When darkness fell, he walked all night again. He was happy to be out-of-doors. "I looked at the stars a lot. I hadn't seen them for quite a while." It was true: He had been locked up for seven years.

On the third day, he again hid during daylight hours. Then finally he heard a brief report on the radio about his escape! It was a short announcement. But he had to keep moving. He walked all night until he found a trailer, where he broke in and stole some wine and food.

Just before sunrise on the sixth day, he saw the lights of a town in the distance. "I decided the heat must be off by now. So when night came, I walked into the town, bought two cans of beer and some sandwiches, and went back to the railroad."

A slow-moving train was coming toward him, and he hopped aboard and rode it. He got off in St. Louis, Missouri, and bought a jacket and a pair of shoes. Then he took a taxicab across the Mississippi River to East St. Louis, Illinois. From a pay phone, he called a friend who agreed to drive him to Edwardsville, Illinois—some twenty-five miles away. He arrived on April 28, and from there, he bought a bus ticket to Chicago.

James Earl Ray had done it. He had escaped from one of the toughest prisons in the United States and had now survived his first week of freedom.

Ray was not an important criminal. He was not a notorious murderer, kidnapper, bank robber, counterfeiter, or mobster. Authorities did not publicize his escape widely and offered only a small, routine fifty-dollar reward for his capture. The FBI did not place Ray on its Most Wanted list or distribute posters bearing his picture to post offices across the country. His escape attracted little attention from the public or the news media. There would be no nationwide manhunt for someone as insignificant as James Earl Ray. If he stayed out of trouble, he might enjoy the rest of his life as a free man.

Martin Luther King was unaware of this event. He had never heard of Ray. They had never met, and King would not have recognized Ray's face. Although the escape of this minor criminal set off no alarm bells, it did set in motion the ticking of a clock that would take almost one year to wind down.

It put Martin Luther King, Jr., and an obscure escaped convict on a deadly collision course.

James Earl Ray was born in Alton, Illinois, on March 10, 1928. His father was an ex-convict who sometimes worked as a manual laborer. He was lazy, often unemployed, and frequently absent from home. He set a poor example for his firstborn son.

James's mother was only nineteen when he was born, and she had eight more children after him. In 1929 the family moved across the Mississippi River to St. Louis, and in 1932 they relocated to the

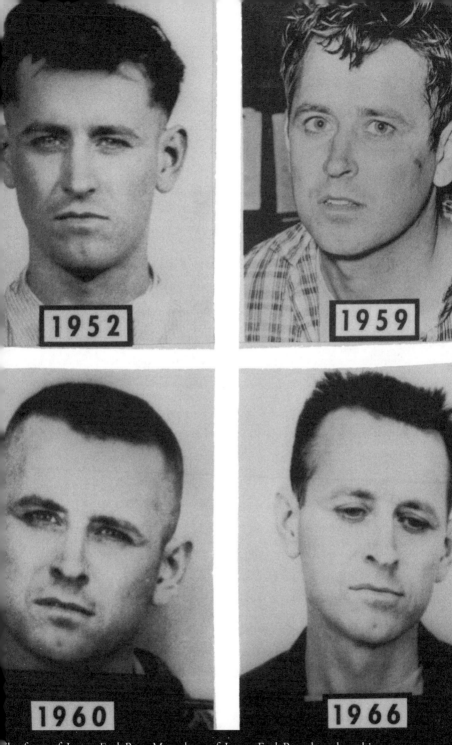

1952

1959

1960

1966

The faces of James Earl Ray: Mug shots of James Earl Ray show how his appearance changed over time.

small town of Ewing, Missouri. James began with disadvantages. His family was poor and lived in primitive conditions. Things were as dismal as they had been at the end of the Civil War. Lowly birth, meager circumstances, bad influences, and his poor education put James Earl Ray on a precarious path from the start.

"Jimmy" Ray was exactly the kind of underprivileged child that Martin Luther King, Jr., wanted to help. He failed and had to repeat the first grade. He did not enjoy school and was often absent. His family was too poor to buy him new shirts, pants, or shoes, and he thought the other children made fun of him because he wore old, patched clothes. A teacher described him cruelly, saying he looked "repulsive." School records described him as dishonest, "seldom if ever polite," and one who "violated all regulations."

When he was fifteen and had not advanced beyond the eighth grade, he dropped out of school. In 1944, when he was sixteen, he got a job at a tannery for a shoe factory, where he learned to dye animal hides. But, almost two years later, he lost that job when the factory downsized after the end of the Second World War.

In February 1946, Ray enlisted in the United States Army. After basic training, where he learned to shoot a rifle, he was shipped out in July to Bremerhaven, Germany, and served as a private in the military police for the American army in Allied-occupied Germany. He was not a good soldier: He got into fights and sold stolen goods. He even served three months in an army stockade for drunkenness and resisting arrest. On December 23, 1948, he was discharged for "ineptness and lack of adaptability to military service."

Back in the United States, Ray needed to earn a living, but he was unmotivated and did not want to work for a paycheck. Instead, he went to California, and in 1949, he committed a burglary and was sentenced to eight months in jail. By this point, Ray had graduated to more violent crimes, committing armed stickups and bank robberies. He and his brothers banded together in a gang of armed thieves, as the whole family was as shiftless and allergic to honest work as he was. Sometimes Ray, one of his brothers, and his uncle (who was the family's inspiration and criminal leader) were even incarcerated in the same prison at the same time. James's uncle passed on his insider knowledge of how to survive and even thrive in prison.

Some families take pride in establishing a multigenerational tradition of farming, of military service, of mastering a trade, or of pursuing education. The Rays took perverse pride in their criminality, passing it down from one generation to the next. Like his relatives, Ray had street smarts, always with an eye for "the main chance." In an era that made folk heroes out of Bonnie and Clyde, the most ruthless and celebrated bank robbers in the South, the Ray family was content to create a legacy of petty crimes of opportunity, deception, fraud, and burglary.

In 1952, James committed an armed robbery of a Chicago taxi driver, was shot by the police, and served nearly two years at the Illinois State Prison at Pontiac. In September 1954, he was arrested for burglary in Edwardsville, Illinois, and while free on bond in March 1955, he burglarized a U.S. Post Office, stole almost seventy blank postal money orders, and then forged the endorsements to obtain cash or goods. For that crime he was sent to the federal prison at Leavenworth, Kansas, until April 1958.

However, there was one type of crime James Earl Ray had never committed. No evidence suggests that Ray ever participated in political or racial violence or hate crimes. He never singled out a victim because of his or her race, nor was he part of the Ku Klux Klan. Like millions of poor whites in the pre-WWII South, Ray had grown up with the prejudices common to his time, class, and region. But he was not known to be a warrior battling on the front lines of racism, fighting against desegregation or equal rights. On those issues, he stood on the sidelines. Ray was a believer in just one cause: grabbing a quick buck in the easiest way possible. Ray had been arrested plenty of times. But there were many other times when he had gotten away with it. To this day, Ray remains a suspect in a number of unsolved bank robberies.

It would be hard to find a man who was less like Martin Luther King, Jr., than James Earl Ray. From birth, King was everything that Ray was not: highly intelligent, ambitious, well-educated, religious, charismatic, eloquent, hardworking, and committed to a moral cause bigger than himself. That commitment had made King into one of the most famous and admired men in the world, and a confidant of the president of the United States. It was as though King and Ray were from different planets.

In October 1959, Ray participated in the armed robbery of a Kroger grocery store in St. Louis, a crime that yielded him little money but had severe consequences. The robbery had netted him and his accomplice just one hundred and twenty dollars—sixty dollars each. Captured immediately and sentenced as a habitual criminal to twenty years in prison at Missouri State Penitentiary at Jefferson City—one year for each pitiful three dollars he had stolen—James Earl Ray seemed destined to sit out the rest of the turbulent 1960s and 1970s on the sidelines, behind bars, and isolated from mainstream American life.

By spring 1967, while still in prison, he had already missed the early achievements of the space program, including the flights of astronauts Alan Shepard and John Glenn; the assassination of President John F. Kennedy in 1963; and the election of President Lyndon B. Johnson in 1964. Languishing year after year in prison, Ray could only watch—but not personally experience—America as it was transformed by pivotal events and social movements: the escalation of the Vietnam War; the civil rights movement; the 1965 assassination of black Muslim leader Malcolm X; the birth of the antiwar movement; and the emergence of the women's rights movement. He was like a fly frozen in amber as the world moved forward.

If James Earl Ray had served out his sentence and been released from prison in 1980, no one would have ever heard of him. By then, he would have been fifty-two years old, and he would have been no more than a bystander to the era, isolated from one of the most event-packed decades in United States history. And he would have been released into a radically changed America.

In 1967, however, his escape catapulted him into the maelstrom of the 1960s. He was thirty-eight when he escaped from Jefferson City. He'd been imprisoned for more than one-third of his life, and he'd served thirteen years in four prisons. His escape had opened up an alternative universe of possibilities and the chance to rewrite his destiny. Now he had a chance to create a new life and to experience firsthand the spirit of his time.

Would he do it? Or would he lapse into his old criminal habits?

To survive on the run, Ray would need, more than anything else, money. Committing more crimes—even behaving suspiciously—might attract law enforcement scrutiny that could land him back in prison. But because there was no nationwide manhunt for him, he would be safe as long as he did nothing to call attention to himself. The popular weekly TV drama *The F.B.I.*, which closed each episode by broadcasting the mug shot of a wanted criminal, was not going to choose him for this notorious honor. Ray was too bland and insignificant.

In fact, James Earl Ray possessed an important trait that proved invaluable in his life of crime. He was a kind of everyman with an average-looking face and a flat, unremarkable personality that was difficult to remember. He didn't stand out. He had a face that could confound a witness. He was the kind of man who failed to make a vivid impression and who, witnesses would often say later, looked just like anybody else.

Still, to avoid exposure, Ray kept moving. He arrived in Chicago on April 30, 1967, and soon found work eighteen miles north in Winnetka, a wealthy lakefront suburb. From May 7 to June 25, he had a job at the Indian Trail restaurant, where one of the owners remembered him as "such a nice man." She described Ray as "quiet, neat, efficient, and so dependable," but also said "he seemed lonely and shy."

This police lineup photo of James Earl Ray was taken early in his criminal career.

Ray had fond memories of his six weeks at the restaurant. "Yes, I had a good job there, and I hated to quit. I was earning far more money than I ever had in my life." He was making the princely sum of one hundred and seventeen dollars a week—nearly as much as the hundred and twenty dollars he stole in the armed robbery that got him a twenty-year prison sentence! But he was afraid to remain at the Indian Trail too long, fearing the FBI would discover that he was using a false name and someone else's social security number. So he quit to keep moving, and drove to Montreal, Canada, in July 1967, where he adopted a different false name: Eric Starvo Galt.

He stayed in Canada for a little more than a month, but then went south to Birmingham, Alabama, arriving on August 25, 1967. There he bought a white Mustang car, and, in September, applied for a driver's license under his new false name. What he would do with his new identity remained to be seen.

Ray next went to Mexico, passing through Acapulco on the way to Puerto Vallarta, where he stayed from October 19 until mid-November. He posed as a writer, toting a typewriter, notebooks, and camera equipment, and driving a flashy car. Ray enjoyed this time like a vacation. It was cheap to stay in Mexico, so Ray took advantage of his opportunities, visiting many places, socializing with women, and treating locals to rides in his Mustang. After a brief visit to New Orleans, he set off to California, arriving in sunny Los Angeles on November 19, 1967, where he rented a cheap apartment for the next two months.

Like many Americans who drifted to California in the 1960s,

James Earl Ray was trying to reinvent himself. He tried but failed to enter the business of making amateur adult films. He bought good-quality camera equipment, but that scheme went nowhere. Next he enrolled in a mail-order course to learn to be a locksmith, a useful skill for a burglar. He also became obsessed with self-help books, optimistic pop psychology texts that promised their readers new and better lives for the price of a fifty-cent paperback.

At this point, Ray was forty years old. He was a lonely, single man with no ties to a stable community. Instead, he was part of a loose-knit world of bars, clubs, seedy rooming houses, and the people who frequented them. He was a neat but not flashy dresser. He kept himself well groomed. He hated to wear dirty clothes, so he had his garments cleaned once a week at the Home Service Laundry on Hollywood Boulevard. In conversation, he was vague, secretive, and nondescript. He kept his opinions to himself. In appearance and demeanor, he was average in every way. And he shared his life with no one.

Ray also became fascinated by hypnosis. Starting November 27, 1967, he consulted a clinical psychologist, Dr. Mark O. Freeman, who taught him self-hypnosis as a way to increase his self-confidence and his ability to accomplish things.

On the same day, Martin Luther King, Jr., was thinking about grander things. On November 27, 1967, he announced plans for a "Poor People's Campaign" in Washington, DC, the following summer. King hoped to unite Americans of all races and from all parts of the country in a common cause to demonstrate for better lives and economic advancement.

James Earl Ray had no interest in cooperation between races. Instead, he volunteered at the George Wallace presidential campaign headquarters in North Hollywood. Wallace was the segregationist Alabama governor who had defied efforts to enroll blacks in the state's schools. He was gearing up to run in the presidential election of 1968. His Hollywood outpost was on a shoestring budget and attracted an oddball following. Ray identified with Wallace's antigovernment, anticommunist, racist, and pro-segregationist views. Ray studied hate literature. He supported the white-power majority government that ruled the African nation of Rhodesia, and he even thought of moving there to become a mercenary soldier.

In December 1967, Ray enrolled in ballroom dancing lessons at the National Dance Studios on Pacific Avenue in Long Beach, California. He learned the rumba, the cha-cha, and various popular dances. But he was socially awkward and did not mix with the other students.

Ray spent Christmas Eve of 1967 alone in Los Angeles. "I don't remember anything about that Christmas," he recalled. "Christmas is for family people. It doesn't mean anything to a loner like me. It's just another day and another night to go to a bar or sit in your room and look at the paper and drink a beer or two and maybe switch on the TV." On New Year's Eve, he drove alone to Las Vegas and watched strangers gamble and play slot machines at casinos. He slept in his car and then drove back to Los Angeles.

Ray seemed content to pursue life on the West Coast. The warm weather and the easygoing lifestyle welcomed people without a past and were attractive to a man who wanted to leave his old life behind.

Until now, nothing about his interests, behavior, or activities in the eight months between his April prison escape and the end of 1967 suggested that he was on a collision course with Martin Luther King. He was obsessed with himself, not with King. Like so many others dissatisfied with their lives, Ray wanted, in the pop psychology language of the day, to "find himself." He wanted his old self to disappear—and he wanted to reinvent himself in a new and improved version. It was a common aspiration of many people who went to California in the 1960s. The state became a symbol of new freedom and opportunity, and a haven for lost and troubled souls. Tens of thousands of Americans made the journey there.

By the end of 1967, President Lyndon Johnson was fighting multiple wars simultaneously. In his dream to create what he called the Great Society, he joined the fight for civil rights and against poverty and racism. In Vietnam, he had sent several hundred thousand Americans into battle. And at home, he fought against critics who wanted to end that war. Civil rights demonstrators were no longer the only people who marched in the nation's streets. Now they were joined by young college students who protested United States involvement in Vietnam. Opposition to LBJ was building.

As 1967 drew to a close, no one knew that the New Year would be one of the most explosive years in American history. And for Lyndon B. Johnson, Martin Luther King, Jr., and James Earl Ray, 1968 would change their lives forever.

A VERY BAD YEAR

For the United States, 1968 began with chaos. North Vietnam launched a surprise military attack to coincide with Tet, the Vietnamese New Year. The enemy struck at major points across South Vietnam, including behind American lines, and even penetrated the United States embassy in Saigon, the capital. Although the Tet Offensive was crushed, the attack stunned the American military and it increased public skepticism about the chances for success of the war effort. It also intensified Martin Luther King's antiwar stance, and it hurt President Johnson's popularity.

For James Earl Ray, 1968 began with introspection. On January 4, he inaugurated the New Year by consulting another hypnotist. This one offered him a "mental profile" and gave him more self-help books for his collection.

The new year also began with an attempt to earn an honest paycheck. On January 15, 1968, he enrolled at the International School of Bartending on Sunset Boulevard. In the six-week course, he would learn the recipes for at least 112 cocktails. Instructor Tomas Reyes Lau recalled Ray as a good student, "a nice fellow with a slight

Southern accent, very intelligent, with the ability to develop this type of service."

A few days after enrolling, Ray booked a room at the low-rent St. Francis Hotel on Hollywood Boulevard.

On February 1, 1968, in Memphis, Tennessee, two city trash collectors died in a terrible accident, crushed by the compactor inside their own garbage truck. It did not make national news. It was a local tragedy, one that seemed unlikely to resonate outside Memphis. Nothing suggested that the accident would have worldwide repercussions. But, like a stone skipping across the water of a still lake, this event sent out ripples that would reach far beyond Memphis.

It would touch Martin Luther King, Jr., in a way that no one could have imagined.

Back in California, Ray completed his bartending course on March 2. He posed with Tommy Lau, holding his graduation certificate. At the ceremony, a photographer closed in to take a photograph. Ray tensed. It was one of the cardinal rules for an escaped criminal: Never pose for pictures. Just before the photographer snapped the shutter, Ray closed his eyes tight and held them shut until after the picture was taken. It was an old con man's trick to make it harder for anyone who saw the photo to recognize him.

Although Ray continued to study his psychology and self-improvement books, he wanted more than mental growth—he also wanted to physically look better, or, at least, different. In February, he decided to have plastic surgery. He wanted a rhinoplasty to give

James Earl Ray made himself difficult to identify by closing his eyes for this bartending school graduation photo.

his nose a narrower, more refined shape and make it less pointed. He also considered having his ears pinned back. He thought they stuck out too much.

On March 5, Ray visited a Los Angeles plastic surgeon, Dr. Russell Hadley. Ray handed over two hundred dollars in cash (probably gotten from minor criminal activities) for the operation, and the doctor performed the rhinoplasty immediately. Ray told him that any cosmetic work on his ears would have to wait until he had more money. As Ray recalled, "I went back to the hotel room and while the nose was still numb, I removed the tape and pushed the nose to the other side and down to change the way the doctor had shaped it in case he remembered me." Such squeezing and reshaping must have been agonizing. But it must have worked, because later, Dr. Hadley—like so many people who had interacted with Ray—remembered almost nothing about him. As Hadley said, "Faces are my business. But what amazes me is that, try as I might, I cannot remember anything at all about Eric S. Galt."

Ray had achieved his objective: to be unrecognizable. He believed that a criminal should have a face "which nobody can describe," and, as it turned out, nobody could.

In the middle of March 1968, Martin Luther King, Jr., flew to Los Angeles. It was the first time that he and James Earl Ray had been in the same city. On March 16, King spoke at Disneyland. The newspapers publicized his visit. But Ray made no effort to see him.

The next day, on March 17—St. Patrick's Day—King delivered a sermon. His friend Reverand James Lawson had made a special request. Would King please fly to Memphis the next day and speak at an evening rally? The death of the two black garbage collectors there in February had provoked the city's sanitation workers to go on strike for higher pay, better benefits, and safer working conditions. Because they were black, Memphis was treating them as second-class citizens. A visit from King, explained Lawson, would help their cause. This was more than a labor dispute. It had become a rallying cry for civil rights. King agreed to come. He couldn't say no to the people in Memphis, to people who needed him.

On the same day, James Earl Ray did an odd and unexpected thing. He filled out change of address cards at the St. Francis Hotel. He packed all of his possessions—his portable television, his transistor radio, his camera equipment, his clothes, his personal papers, his pistol, and his books, including his much-valued self-help guides—into the trunk of his white Mustang. Then he got in the car, revved up the engine, and started driving east. Bizarrely, Ray's destination was the city of Selma, Alabama, a hot spot of the civil rights movement, where marchers were brutally attacked on Bloody Sunday in March 1965 when they tried to cross the Edmund Pettus Bridge.

It was curious that Ray's decision to leave California coincided with King's trip to the West Coast. On March 17, 1968, something must have happened to James Earl Ray. He had been an aimless wanderer, avoiding recapture and a return to prison. Now he was a man on a mission. It was as if he had been slumbering for a year, in a kind of suspended animation while he pursued various oddball quests: bartending school, dance lessons, hypnosis, self-help books, plastic surgery, a mail-order locksmithing course, lounging in bars, promoting George Wallace's presidential campaign, and cheap amateur photography and filmmaking. Ray's vagabond lifestyle included interstate travel to Illinois, Missouri, Louisiana, Alabama, California, and more, plus foreign travel to Mexico and Canada. It is likely that he also committed a string of bank robberies along the way.

Like a film actor, Ray did all this using a collection of false names, alternative identities, deceptive stories, and various personal looks. Ray tried on new personas as easily as another man might try on a new suit of clothes. He presented an odd mix of habits and appearances. In a rumpled flannel shirt and long hair, he resembled a manual laborer. In a neat suit and tie with his hair combed back, and wearing black plastic eyeglasses, he could impersonate a businessman or a professor. Like a chameleon, he blended into his surroundings, a man of many faces. Through the years, so many people had forgotten exactly what he looked like, or what he said. For much of his life, Ray had been a most forgettable man.

That all came to an end on Sunday, March 17, 1968. Like a caged homing pigeon released to the sky, or a hibernating animal awakened by nature's call, he responded to an inner signal that only he could hear and that would direct his movements over the next three weeks. It was as though a silent, invisible alarm inside him had rung, summoning him to the South.

What had motivated James Earl Ray to abandon his easy California life and drive across the country?

He had decided to kill Dr. Martin Luther King, Jr.

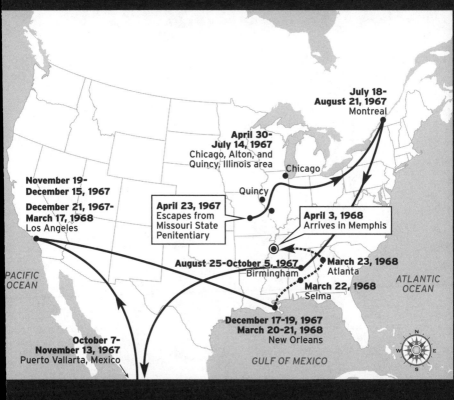

This is Ray's complicated and random-seeming route leading up to the assassination.
His movements after March 17 are marked with a dotted line.

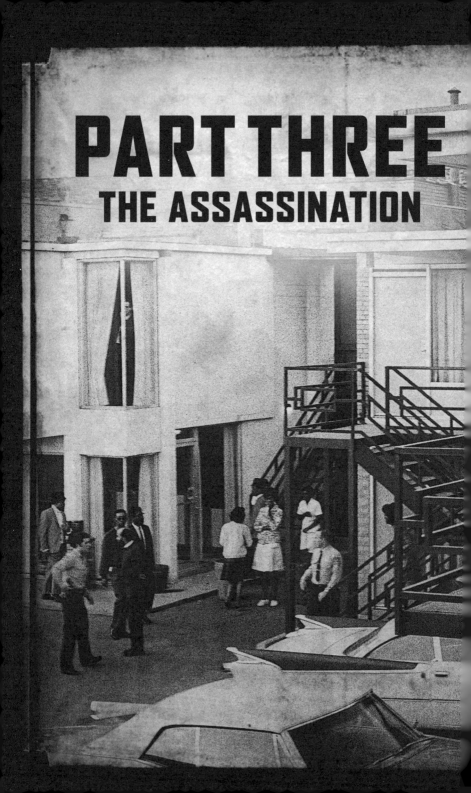

PART THREE
THE ASSASSINATION

PLANNING A MURDER

James Earl Ray was an unlikely assassin. He was no trained hit man. He had never killed or even tried to kill a man in his life. Nor was he an expert marksman with pistols or rifles. There is no evidence that he had escaped from prison with the intention to murder Dr. King, or anyone else.

While Ray drove across America, Martin Luther King was in Memphis to speak on March 18 to the striking sanitation workers at the Mason Temple. To protest their dehumanizing working conditions, the men had been picketing. They had carried cardboard signs that said I AM A MAN. That evening, King spoke to them about economic justice, about equal access to jobs and pay. He had no idea that even as he spoke, day by day, hour by hour, a stranger was driving across America to find him and kill him. King even agreed to come back to Memphis in a few days, on the 22nd, to lead a march through the streets.

But around midnight on March 21, King was stranded in Birmingham, Alabama. A freak snowstorm had paralyzed Memphis and forced the cancellation of the march the next day.

On March 22, after driving for four days, James Earl Ray arrived in Selma, Alabama. He checked into the Flamingo Hotel, located just a few blocks from the Edmund Pettus Bridge, the site of the Bloody Sunday violence. By reading the local newspapers and watching the news on television, Ray could keep track of King's schedule. Although King was supposed to speak in Selma that day, Ray was not ready to take action. He needed equipment and a plan.

On March 23, King spoke at a rally for the Poor People's Campaign in Augusta, Georgia, a few hundred miles from Selma. This was to be a rally for people of all races—including blacks and whites. King believed that all poor people were united by their poverty and shared a common cause. He seemed to be moving from championing civil rights to a more universal call to help all disadvantaged people. A march in Washington, DC, would illustrate this.

On that same day, Ray moved on toward Atlanta, King's hometown. Ray arrived there the next day, March 24, and checked into a cheap rooming house in a seedy part of town. The rent was $1.50 per night, and he paid in advance for a one-week stay. He wanted time to stalk King and to obtain information on his schedule and movements. For the next three days, from March 25 to 28, while Martin Luther King, Jr., was in New York and New Jersey, Ray remained at the Atlanta rooming house, waiting for King's return.

On March 28, King flew to Memphis. This was his second attempt to lead a march in support of the striking sanitation workers after the protest he had planned to lead there on March 22 was canceled. But it turned out to be a disaster. A group of young radicals

Up to fifteen thousand people, including a thousand sanitation workers, assembled outside Mason Temple in Memphis, Tennessee, in preparation for a protest march. Many of their signs read I AM A MAN.

who were called "The Invaders" disrupted the event and began smashing shop windows.

King shouted to Ralph Abernathy: "There's violence breaking out!"

For more than a decade, Abernathy had been Martin Luther King, Jr.'s closest advisor, confidant, and partner in the leadership of the civil rights movement. King was the public face of the cause while Abernathy was more of a behind-the-scenes influence. They were inseparable; Abernathy was like a brother to King, an alter ego. They had shared the ups and downs of the movement, the hardships of life on the road. If you saw Martin Luther King, Jr., you usually saw Ralph Abernathy at his side. Each man made the other stronger. Some people even thought that Abernathy should have shared in the Nobel Peace Prize King received.

King knew he could not be present during a violent demonstration. That would undermine the reputation he had earned for seeking justice through peaceful means. He, Abernathy, and a few others left the march and took refuge at a hotel. It was an embarrassing failure. King wanted to get out of Memphis.

In the meantime, James Earl Ray had narrowed down a plan.

He decided that he would not use his pistol to assassinate King. Using a handgun would require him to get close. That meant witnesses. And it risked capture or even death at the hands of King's enraged followers. He did not possess the proper weapon to do it.

So, on March 29, Ray drove more than one hundred miles from Atlanta, Georgia, to Birmingham, Alabama, and visited the Aeromarine Supply Company, a sporting goods store. After inspecting several weapons, he selected a Remington Gamemaster .243-caliber, bolt-action hunting rifle. Ray also asked for a telescopic scope and ammunition. The total cost was $248.59—a relative value of over a thousand dollars today. A customer at the store told Ray that he had picked out quite a rifle and asked what he planned to hunt with it. Using the false name of Harvey Lowmeyer, he paid for it in cash. The clerk told Ray to come back later and pick up the rifle after an employee had time to mount the scope on the weapon. He did.

It was easy to buy a firearm in those days. Gun sales were not as regulated by the government as they are today, and buying one was as easy as purchasing a power drill, or a chain saw, or any other tool at a hardware store. In fact, many hardware stores and department stores sold firearms. In the more laid-back gun culture of the

Aeromarine Supply Company, where Ray bought his rifle.

1960s, a customer did not even have to present identification. The store and the manufacturer verified and retained only one type of record—the serial number stamped on each firearm shipped to a particular retailer, plus a copy of the sales receipt.

Later that day, Ray called the store back, saying he had made a mistake. He wanted to exchange the rifle for a more powerful one. He claimed that his brother had told him that he had bought the wrong gun. That was fine with Aeromarine—it meant that this customer would probably upgrade to a more expensive weapon. However, they were about to close and asked if he could come back tomorrow to get a different rifle.

So on the morning of March 30, Ray returned to the Aeromarine store to exchange his rifle. He examined another one, a Remington Gamemaster model 760 hunting rifle. It fired a powerful .30-caliber bullet that was twice as heavy as the bullets for the rifle he had selected the day before. That meant the rifle had more killing power.

Unlike the rifle he had returned, which required the shooter to operate a manual bolt to eject a fired round and load a fresh one into the chamber, the model 760 was a pump-action that did not require the shooter to operate a manual bolt. This feature allowed a shooter to fire faster and keep his eye on the target. Ray chose a Redfield adjustable scope. He paid for the more expensive weapon and was told to come back at 3:00 p.m. to pick it up, again to give the shop employee time to mount the scope on the rifle. Ray also took two boxes of ammunition that held twenty rounds each. He drove his purchases back to his Atlanta rooming house.

The same day, on March 30, King flew from Memphis to Atlanta,

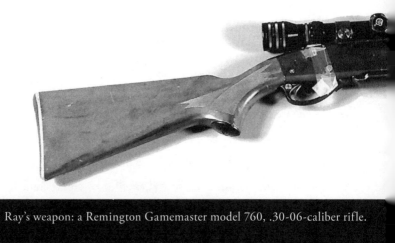

Ray's weapon: a Remington Gamemaster model 760, .30-06-caliber rifle.

where he held a staff meeting at his headquarters, Ebenezer Baptist Church. He vowed to return to Memphis a third time to lead a successful march there, but his aides rebelled. Several argued that he should not return, believing that Memphis was a distraction from their other work. Why go back? Hadn't he done enough there already? Going back only invited another disaster. Then King and his advisors argued about the planned Poor People's March. Some of them said it was a bad idea, and that it would fail and hurt the cause. King got frustrated and walked out of the meeting. He wanted to get out of town.

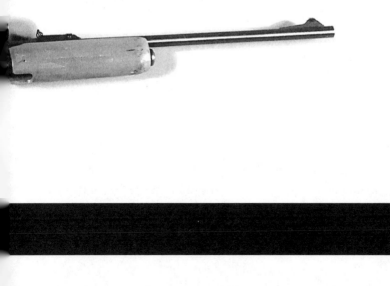

MOMENTOUS DAYS

The next day, on March 31, Martin Luther King, Jr., delivered a sermon at the famous National Cathedral, a huge neo-Gothic church, in Washington, DC. He preached about more than civil rights. After the service, he said: "I would like to mention another thing closely related to racism—poverty." He reminded people that the Poor People's Campaign was coming to Washington, DC, that summer. About Vietnam he said: "I am convinced that it is one of the most unjust wars that has ever been fought in the history of the world."

Later that night, in a historic televised announcement, President Johnson spoke to the American people. The text of the president's speech had been a closely guarded secret. When he began speaking to the television cameras in the Oval Office at 9:00 p.m. EST on March 31, even his closest aides did not know what he was going to say. During the speech, LBJ dropped a bombshell: "I shall not seek, and I will not accept, the nomination of my party for another term as your president." Controversy over the Vietnam War had driven him from the presidency.

March 31 had been a momentous day, filled with big events. Martin Luther King had given his last sermon. Lyndon Johnson had withdrawn from the presidential race of 1968. And, just one day earlier, James Earl Ray had bought a rifle.

COUNTDOWN TO MEMPHIS

The next day, on April 1, the *Atlanta Constitution* newspaper reported that in a few days, King would return to Memphis. Reading the newspaper was the best way for Ray to keep track of King's movements, so he probably read the story.

At 10:00 a.m., he dropped off some laundry at the cleaners. He had grown impatient waiting for King. Martin Luther King's schedule was unpredictable and it often changed at the last minute. Ray also might have decided that Atlanta was not a good place for an assassination. A white man in a light-colored Mustang would stand out and attract attention in King's neighborhood. And a sniper attack on King as he arrived for church or left after the service would have to be carried out in daylight. That plan was too risky, and it might be difficult to escape.

Ray decided to follow King to Memphis. On April 2, Ray packed the rifle and some of his possessions into the trunk of his car. He left some things behind in his room, including his TV. Driving west out of Atlanta, he took the highway heading toward Tennessee.

Martin Luther King, Jr., spent the night of April 2 at his home in Atlanta with his wife, Corrie. The Abernathys came over for dinner, and Martin and Ralph talked about their flight to Memphis the next morning.

It was King's last night with his family.

A GREAT DAY—
"I WOULD LIKE TO LIVE"

On the morning of April 3, Ralph Abernathy picked up King at his home and drove to the Atlanta airport. Once they boarded the plane, the flight crew announced that there would be a slight delay before they got airborne. Someone had phoned in a bomb threat. The plane would have to be searched. King was not alarmed. Threats like this were routine and almost business as usual for him. White racists may have bombed black homes and churches, but they had not yet figured out how to blow a plane out of the sky. Martin joked to Ralph: "Well, it looks like they won't kill me this flight."

Abernathy reassured him: "Nobody's going to kill you, Martin."

It was King's third trip to Memphis in three weeks, and his third attempt to lead a march to support the striking sanitation workers. The unseasonal, freak snowstorm had prevented the first one. Rioting and violence had ruined the second. King's aides had objected to these multiple visits. It was almost as if, via a series of ill omens, fate had warned him to stay away from Memphis.

April 3, 1968. Martin Luther King, Jr., arrives at Memphis airport with colleagues (left to right) Andrew Young, Ralph Abernathy, and Bernard Lee. They planned a protest march in support of striking Memphis sanitation workers.

When King landed, his regular driver in Memphis, Reverand Solomon Jones, picked him and Abernathy up at the airport. Jones always drove a white Cadillac that a local funeral home loaned for King's convenience whenever he was in town. Jones knew where to go—the Lorraine Motel, a black-owned business that rented rooms to blacks as well as whites. It was King's favorite place to stay whenever he came to town.

Meanwhile, James Earl Ray was still on the road, closing the distance to Memphis.

At the Lorraine Motel, King's entourage awaited him: James Bevel, James Orange, Jesse Jackson, Hosea Williams, Chauncey Eskridge, Bernard Lee, Dorothy Cotton, Andrew Young, and others. A South African documentary filmmaker, Joseph Louw, and a black *New York Times* reporter, Earl Caldwell, were also there. King's brother, A. D. King, and Georgia Davis, a young state senator from Kentucky, were expected later.

King convened a strategy meeting at Reverand James Lawson's Centenary United Methodist Church. The city had obtained an injunction, or court order, against the march, arguing that after the riot last time, it was too dangerous. The city did not want to take the risk that King might be harmed. Back in his room at the Lorraine Motel, King met with his lawyer, Lucius Burch, to discuss how to fight the city's injunction. King told the lawyer that the march was vital. Burch left to prepare the documents necessary to oppose the injunction.

At a fire department station within sight of the Lorraine Motel, two black Memphis police officers were on duty with orders to keep

Taking a break from organizing the march in support of strikers, on April 3, 1968, King and his aides gather on the balcony of the Lorraine Motel in Memphis, Tennessee. From left to right: Hosea Williams, Jesse Jackson, Dr. King, and Ralph Abernathy.

an eye on King. They were not there to spy on him or to gather information to use against him. Their assignment was more benign: to make sure that nobody created any trouble or disturbances. The city wanted the visit to go smoothly. The policemen took up their positions. From one of the windows, they could see the front door to King's room. Soon, the policemen were ordered to leave their observation post and go to King's next stop, to be in position there before he arrived.

Martin Luther King had agreed to speak at a big public rally that night at the Mason Temple. During the afternoon, dark, threatening skies formed over the city. By 7:00 p.m., heavy rain and howling winds seemed to shake the rafters at the Lorraine Motel and the Temple.

James Earl Ray arrived in Memphis that day around 7:15 p.m. He drove his Mustang into the parking lot of the New Rebel Motel at 3466 Lamar Avenue, on the southwestern edge of the city. An outdoor neon sign of a Civil War colonel paid homage to the old Confederate States of America. Ray checked in, went to his room, and settled in for the evening. Having found shelter from the storm, he had no intention of going out with his rifle tonight.

Across town at the Lorraine Motel, Martin Luther King, like James Earl Ray, did not want to leave the comfort of his hotel room and venture out into the storm. King was tired. He did not feel well. And he was at a low point in his life. He was worn out from the struggle, and he questioned whether he was still a worthy or effective leader of the movement. Many black leaders argued that his opposition to the Vietnam War had distracted him from his main purpose and hurt the civil rights movement. Younger rivals, impatient with his tactics of nonviolence, advocated more radical methods. And many in his own inner circle doubted the wisdom of the Poor People's Campaign that he wanted to lead in Washington that summer. They judged it too ambitious, too unfocused, and doomed to fail.

King told Ralph Abernathy that the last thing he wanted to do tonight was leave the motel and make a public appearance: "Ralph, I want you to go and speak for me tonight." Abernathy knew he was not as charismatic a personality or as electrifying a speaker as his longtime friend, and he did not want to stand in the spotlight for King. Abernathy suggested that they send Jesse Jackson, one of Martin's energetic young aides from Chicago who craved public attention. King said no: "Nobody else can speak for me. I want you to go."

Abernathy agreed to do it. Arriving at the Mason Temple at 8:30 p.m., he was shocked to find three thousand people clamoring to see Dr. King. The crowd included the two undercover policemen from the firehouse. Before King arrived, the policemen were warned that they had been spotted and that, for their own safety, they should leave the temple. Ralph called the Lorraine Motel and implored King to change his mind: "Martin, all the television networks are lined up, waiting for you. This speech will be broadcast nationwide. You need to deliver it. Besides, the people who are here want you, not me."

"Okay," he said, "I'll come."

King arrived at the Mason Temple at 9:00 p.m. The storm, the anticipation of the crowd, and King's late arrival all combined to create a dramatic atmosphere. As Ralph Abernathy had done on countless prior occasions, he rose to introduce his friend and recounted their friendship and highlights of their work. King then got up and told the crowd, "Ralph Abernathy is the best friend that I have in the world."

King said the reason he had come was bigger than a labor dispute between the city and its garbage collectors. The strike symbolized the civil rights movement. "Something is happening in Memphis. Something is happening in our world. . . . The nation is sick, trouble is in the land." This, King said, was a struggle for freedom. "The masses of people are rising up . . . the cry is always the same: We want to be free!"

King remembered how lucky he was to be here tonight, and how lucky he was to be alive at all. His mind went back ten years.

"You know, several years ago, I was in New York autographing the first book that I had written. And while sitting there . . . a demented black woman came up. The only question I heard from her was 'Are you Martin Luther King?' And I was looking down writing, and I said, 'Yes!' The next minute I felt something beating on my chest. Before I knew it I had been stabbed . . . I was rushed to Harlem Hospital . . . and that blade had gone through, and the X-rays revealed that the tip of the blade was on the edge of my aorta, the main artery. And once that's punctured, you drown in your own blood—that's the end of you. It came out in the *New York Times* the next morning, that if I had merely sneezed, I would have died."

While recovering from his injuries, King had received letters at the hospital from the president of the United States, the vice president, and other important leaders. But now he recalled another letter, one that

"came from a little girl, a young girl who was a student at the White Plains High School . . . and I'll never forget it. It said simply, 'Dear Dr. King: I am a ninth-grade student at the White Plains High School. She said while it should not matter, I would like to mention that I am a white girl. I read in the paper of your misfortune, and of your suffering. And I read that if you had sneezed, you would have died. And I'm simply writing you to say that I'm so happy that you didn't sneeze.'"

A decade later her words still touched him.

Once again, King thought back to that terrible night on September 20, 1958, when he had been so close to dying.

"And I want to say tonight, I want to say that I, too, am happy that I didn't sneeze. Because if I had sneezed, I wouldn't have been around here in 1960, when students all over the South started sitting-in at lunch counters." If he had sneezed, he continued, he wouldn't have been around in 1962, when blacks in Albany, Georgia, decided to "straighten their backs up"; he wouldn't have been alive in 1963, when the black people of Birmingham, Alabama, "aroused the conscience of this nation, and brought into being the Civil Rights Bill"; he would not have spoken in 1963 at the Lincoln Memorial to tell Americans about his dream; he would not have been in Selma, Alabama, to lead the movement there. And if he had sneezed, he would not be in Memphis tonight.

Then he looked to the future. "Well, I don't know what will happen now. We've got some difficult days ahead. But it really doesn't matter with me now. Because I've been to the mountaintop."

King confided that he relished life: "Like anybody, I would like to live a long life. Longevity has its place. But I'm not concerned about that now. I just want to do God's will. And he's allowed me to go up to the mountain. And I've looked over. And I've seen the Promised Land."

King was invoking the Old Testament saga of Moses, who led his people through the wilderness on a difficult and historic journey from slavery to freedom. From a mountaintop, Moses had sighted a new home for his followers. But at the end of this journey, God chose not to allow Moses to enter the Promised Land himself, only to let him see it from a distance.

So King cautioned his audience, "I may not get there with you. But I want you to know tonight, that we, as a people, will get to the Promised Land."

King brought the speech to a rousing conclusion in which he seemed to unburden himself from earthly cares:

"So I'm happy tonight.

"I'm not worried about anything.

"I'm not fearing any man."

But Martin Luther King should have feared one man.

He had no idea the shadow of death that had stalked him for ten years was again drawing near. Soon, King would be in more danger than he had been since the day Izola Curry almost killed him. James Earl Ray lurked with his rifle just a few miles away, sitting out the ferocious storm, taking shelter in a room at the New Rebel Motel. Ray might have been watching King right then, sprawled on his bed while viewing the speech live on a black-and-white television set. If he was, King's words fell on deaf ears. King's celebration of life did not deter Ray's mission of death. It did not soften Ray's heart or dissuade him from doing what he had come to Memphis to do.

I may not get there with you. But I want you to know tonight, that we, as a people, will et to the Promised Land." Martin Luther King's last public appearance, the evening of pril 3, 1968, in Memphis, Tennessee.

Tomorrow, Ray decided, he would begin hunting Martin Luther King.

More than Abraham Lincoln, more than John F. Kennedy, Martin Luther King, Jr., had spent years under the continuous threat of violence. But he persevered and exhibited great personal courage as he went about his work. King was one of the bravest, most fearless figures in American history.

Menace and danger had become constant companions. It was as though, in the last dying gasp of the racist Old South, a century's worth of hatred and vitriol was now aimed at him. If even President Kennedy could not be protected from an assassin, how, King wondered, could he be spared that fate? The only surprise was that no one had succeeded in killing him already.

At the Mason Temple, Martin Luther King, Jr., had spoken for an hour and a half. To conclude the speech, King uttered a prophetic exclamation: "Mine eyes have seen the glory of the Lord!" Drained, he appeared to stagger away from the microphone, almost collapsing into the arms of Ralph Abernathy. On a night when he was ill, tired, did not want to speak at all, and had no prewritten remarks or notes, he had risen to the occasion. It was as though he poured all he ever was, all he had ever seen and done, into this one speech. Ralph Abernathy, who had seen King give hundreds of speeches, knew it better than anyone: "He was at the height of his powers. I never saw him better." It was the most wondrous, luminous speech he ever gave, surpassing even the August 1963 speech at the Lincoln Memorial.

And it was to be his last.

THE LAST DAY

On the morning of April 4, James Earl Ray put on a suit and tie. Dressed like a respectable businessman, he went out for breakfast. He bought a copy of the Memphis *Commercial Appeal* newspaper, which included coverage of Martin Luther King's speech from the previous night. The paper reported that King would remain in town for several more days because he planned to lead another march in Memphis on April 8. The newspaper also published photographs of King taken at the Lorraine Motel. One picture showed the entrance to his room—with the number 306 plainly visible on the door. Now, from either the morning newspaper or from TV coverage the previous night, Ray knew not only where King was staying in Memphis, but the exact room.

Martin Luther King awoke early on the morning of April 4. He had an 8:00 a.m. meeting with his aides and advisors before the court hearing that would decide whether he would be allowed to lead his next march. King spent part of the afternoon in meetings, including a failed negotiation with the so-called Invaders, the group of local young militants who had disrupted, with vandalism and violence, King's most recent attempt to lead a march through Memphis. That disaster was the reason King was back in Memphis now. The conversation went nowhere, and King found them disrespectful and threatening. He threw the Invaders out of his room.

That afternoon, Ray decided to drive over to King's motel. The big, colorful sign outside the Lorraine made the place impossible to miss. He wanted to scout the neighborhood for possible vantage points from which he could place King under surveillance, and then take a shot at him from a safe distance. After a while he found himself on South Main Street, a block away from the Lorraine. He spotted a rooming house at 422-½ South Main. It did not even have a name, just a sign above the entrance that advertised rooms for rent. The Lorraine Motel looked to be less than one hundred yards behind this rooming house, and its windows might offer a good view of King's room.

Ray parked his Mustang in front of the rooming house and went inside. He asked the manager if she had any vacancies. He would be staying a week, Ray told her, and she led him to room 8, which included a kitchen. But he did not care about amenities. Only the view. And this room was on the wrong side of the building. Facing west, it looked out onto Main Street and offered no view of the Lorraine. Ray rejected the room, giving the excuse that he wasn't going to be doing any cooking.

The manager took him to 5B, on the second floor of the east side of the building. It was a cramped little room, lit only by a bare lightbulb that hung from the ceiling. It didn't even have a

The entrance to Ray's rooming house, viewed from South Main Street. The back of the building looks over the Lorraine Motel.

bathroom, meaning he would have to use the filthy shared one down the hall.

But this room had what he wanted. A window that faced the Lorraine Motel. "This'll do just fine," Ray said. He signed his name as John Willard and paid her $8.50 for a week's rent.

After Ray checked into the no-name rooming house and stood alone in his sad little room, he took in his surroundings. He approached the window. He could see it all now—the big, open, paved parking

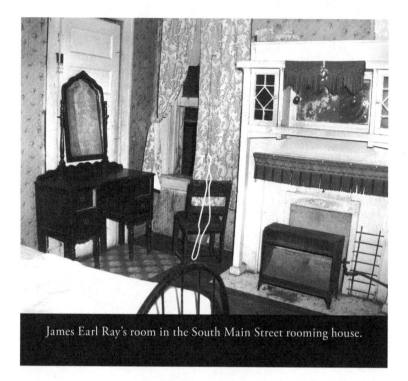

James Earl Ray's room in the South Main Street rooming house.

lot, the long balcony and railings that ran along the length of the building, the numbered room doors. Then he saw it. The door to room 306.

It didn't take Ray long to see that something was wrong. The angle was bad. In order to shoot Dr. King, Ray would have to lean out the window, point his rifle at a sharp angle, and expose himself to possible witnesses. Ray was dismayed to discover that the room he had selected was not the perfect sniper's nest after all. It would not be easy to assassinate King from here.

He could ask for a different room, one with a better view of King's. But that might make the manager suspicious. Ray's trademark behavior throughout his criminal life was never to call too

Detail of Ray's Rooming House and Eventual Escape Route

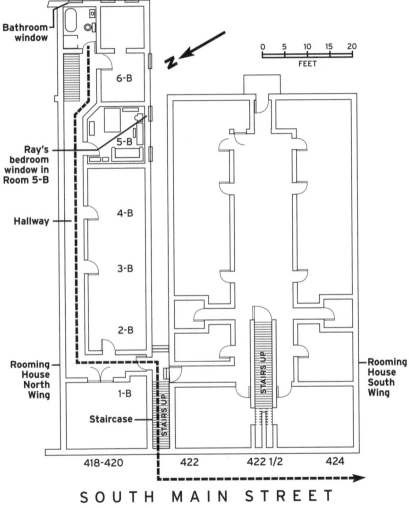

Bathroom window

6-B

5-B

Ray's bedroom window in Room 5-B

Hallway

4-B

3-B

2-B

Rooming House North Wing

1-B

Staircase

Rooming House South Wing

STAIRS UP

STAIRS UP

STAIRS UP

0 5 10 15 20
FEET

N

418-420   422   422 1/2   424

SOUTH MAIN STREET

much attention to himself. Still, he wondered if the view from the shared bathroom at the east end of the hallway might be better.

It was a short walk from room 5B to the bathroom. Ray stepped inside and closed the door. It had a lock. That was a good sign. No one could disturb him in there. Ray approached the window. It was partly open, and an aluminum-framed window screen kept out the flies.

He punched out the screen, and it floated to the ground. He tried to raise the window to give himself more room to maneuver with the rifle. It was stuck. He pulled up hard, but it would not budge. Ray peered through the gap between the top of the sill and the bottom of the window frame.

This small bathroom window had an unobstructed view of Martin Luther King's front door and the balcony outside his room. King would be in range every time he left or returned to the Lorraine Motel. And that balcony was the only route to the room—King would *have* to walk that way. And even though Ray's bathroom window would not open fully, there was sufficient room to poke a rifle with a telescopic sight through the gap.

Ray eyed the stained white porcelain bathtub along the bathroom's north wall. He got an idea. He stepped into the tub and peered through the window again. This spot offered a superior and even more direct line of sight to King's room. So on the afternoon of April 4, James Earl Ray decided that a stained old tub in the shared bathroom of a shabby rooming house was the perfect hiding place from which to assassinate Martin Luther King, Jr.

The plan was risky. Ray could not sit in the bathroom with his rifle for hours, day and night, waiting for Dr. King to show up.

he shared bathroom down the hall from Ray's room. Standing inside the bathtub,
e could see the balcony outside Martin Luther King's room at the Lorraine Motel. After
he shooting investigators raised the stuck window. A handprint, probably Ray's, is visible
1 the wall.

King's schedule was unpredictable and Ray could only guess what hours he might keep. Other residents at Ray's rooming house would eventually need to use the bathroom and would discover the armed man lurking there. No, Ray would have to watch the Lorraine Motel from the window of his own room. Then, when he spotted King and decided that it was the right moment to shoot him, he would have to leave his room, carry his rifle down the hall, enter the bathroom, lock himself inside, step into the tub, point the rifle out the window, and get King in his sights. There was no guarantee that King would stand still for the time it would take Ray to do all those things. And if someone was using the bathroom at the exact time Ray needed it, he would have to figure out a way to get that person out of there.

It would have been much safer for Ray to shoot King from the privacy of his room. But shooting from the bathroom increased the odds of his success.

The clock that had begun ticking a few weeks ago, the day James Earl Ray had left California, was winding down. It was counting off the final hours.

James Earl Ray was almost ready.

But first he had to go down to the street, unlock his car trunk, and, without being observed, bring the rifle up to his room. At the last minute, however, he decided to buy one final piece of equipment. Ray got into his car and drove to a sporting goods store. Anticipating a few days of surveillance, he wanted a pair of binoculars to keep close watch on King and his entourage until he chose the right moment to strike. Ray did not assume he could just move into the rooming house and, within a few hours, shoot King. That kind of quick success would require an incredible combination of chance and luck. No, like a policeman on a stakeout, Ray expected to be there for a while.

Ray had moved into his room with a little, cheap suitcase and supplies for the duration. If he expected to kill King on April 4, he would have carried nothing up to his room except the rifle and ammunition. He would have left his other possessions in his car. From what Ray could learn from the newspapers and television, he expected King to be at the Lorraine for the next few days, until the morning of the march, on April 8. There would be time.

After Ray returned from the sporting goods store at around 4:30 p.m., he parked his car on South Main Street, about sixty feet south of the entrance to his rooming house. He carried the binoculars up to his room and then went back outside, where he sat in his car for a while. He was probably waiting for pedestrian and road traffic to die down at the end of the workday. Several witnesses, including a woman who was waiting for a ride, noticed him. But there was nothing suspicious about a well-dressed man sitting alone in a car. Half an hour passed. By about 5:00 p.m., Ray popped open the trunk, retrieved the rifle, and, careful to conceal it in its cardboard box wrapped in a blanket, carried it up to his room.

Then he got out his binoculars and began his surveillance.

Ray was not the only one watching Dr. King. From the nearby firehouse, the two policemen who had followed him to the Mason Temple the night before had kept him under watch all day.

A little after 5:00 p.m., Andrew Young arrived at room 201 at the Lorraine Motel with good news. A federal judge had lifted the injunction against the march and had agreed to let them have it in four days, on the morning of Monday, April 8. King and his aides became giddy. Everyone in the room—all of them grown men— began a spontaneous pillow fight! King and his colleagues laughed like children, swatting each other as they swung their pillows through the air. The fight ended. It was time to go to dinner. Martin Luther King and Ralph Abernathy walked up one flight of stairs to room 306 to get ready.

Less than seventy yards away, across the parking lot and behind the retaining wall that separated the Lorraine Motel from the rear of the buildings on South Main Street, James Earl Ray was spying on them.

A long and curious journey had brought Ray to this place. But would his plan work?

Success was not inevitable. Ray did not possess the deadly skills of a professional killer. No, he was an amateur. Anyone could buy a rifle. But not everyone had the skill and temperament to use one to kill a man.

It was getting close to 6:00 p.m. King was hungry, and he was look-ing forward to enjoying a fine, home-cooked Southern soul food dinner at the home of his friend Billy Kyles, a local Memphis minis-ter. King savored home-cooked meals of his favorite dishes prepared to order, relaxing with friends, telling stories, and laughing. In public settings—at rallies, protests, and speeches—Martin Luther King, Jr., put on a somber, serious face and spoke with the intensity of an Old Testament prophet. On public occasions, he had few opportunities to show his sense of humor. Major events exhausted him and could almost drain the life force out of him. Off duty, surrounded by friends around whom he could relax and be himself, Martin loved to laugh.

King was like Abraham Lincoln. Before his presidency, Lincoln rode the Eighth Judicial Circuit in Illinois, traveling from town to town, trying legal cases by day. But at night, he enjoyed himself with a close circle of fellow lawyers and judges. Martin Luther King traveled the civil rights circuit. And he, like Lincoln, enjoyed the camaraderie of the road.

Tonight, King was off the clock, without obligations or speeches to deliver. He could relax after the triumph of last night's "Mountaintop" speech, which would become as famous as his 1963 "I Have a Dream" speech at the Lincoln Memorial. And he wanted to celebrate today's courtroom victory. He was eager to enjoy a fine meal prepared by Billy Kyles's wife. King speculated if she had prepared his favorite dishes. He was impatient, so he asked Ralph Abernathy to find out.

"Call her up and ask what she's serving."

Ralph laughed and asked, "You're not kidding, are you?"

Abernathy called and recited the mouthwatering menu: roast beef, asparagus, cauliflower—and candied yams, pigs' feet, and chitlins. After hearing that, King was very eager to leave for dinner.

***

Later, at 5:50 p.m., three police cars pulled into the driveway of the firehouse a block from the Lorraine Motel. The ten men from Tactical Unit 10—a mixed force of Memphis policemen and sheriffs—were on a break. It was common for policemen to hang out at local fire stations when they wanted to relax. They got out of their vehicles and walked inside.

In the Lorraine Motel parking lot, several members of King's group were already hanging out, waiting for Doc to come down. In a few minutes they would pile into their cars and drive to dinner. King emerged from his room. From his perch on the balcony, he looked down at the parking lot and bantered with his friends who were milling around below him. They could all leave for dinner as soon as he and Ralph Abernathy were ready to go.

King spotted Ben Branch, his friend and a popular bandleader, and asked him to sing him a tune later that evening. "I want him to play my favorite song, 'Precious Lord, Take My Hand,'" King said. "Sing it for me real pretty," he told Branch.

King then turned around and walked back into his room. He asked Abernathy: "You ready to go?"

"Let me put my cologne on," Ralph said.

"Okay," said King, "I'll wait on the balcony."

King stepped outside.

James Earl Ray watched him through his binoculars.

Ray had been prepared to wait several days for an opportunity like this. He was lucky. He had only had to wait a few hours.

Martin Luther King was on the balcony, out in the open. He was not surrounded by bodyguards or aides. He was alone. And he was standing still.

James Earl Ray made an instantaneous decision.

"Now," a voice inside him commanded, "do it right now." Adrenaline coursed through him. He put the binoculars down and reached for his rifle.

Ray had to get to the bathroom fast. If he waited too long, King might start walking along the balcony and descend the staircase to the parking lot.

Ray stuffed his belongings into his zippered nylon suitcase, not wanting to leave any evidence behind. He got almost all of his possessions, but overlooked the carrying strap for his new binoculars, which was left on the floor.

Ray wrapped a blanket around the cardboard box containing his rifle. Carrying the bag and the rifle, he stepped into the hall, dashed to the bathroom, and locked the door. No one saw him. Ray stepped into the tub and peered out the window. King was still there.

One of the residents of the rooming house wanted to use the bathroom. He walked to the door and tried to open it. It was locked. He knocked. No one answered. Another resident told him that the new guy was in there.

Ray pointed the rifle out the window and rested it on the sill to steady it. Its weight made a slight memory mark on the wood. He aimed toward the balcony. He pressed the butt of the stock firmly against his right shoulder. He wrapped the fingers of his right hand

The sniper's nest: This is a police photo of the view from the bathroom window from which James Earl Ray shot Martin Luther King, Jr. King's room, 306 (marked "A") is visible slightly to the right of center. "B" shows where King was standing.

around the grip. He inserted his index finger inside the trigger guard. He peered into the telescopic scope and adjusted the rifle until he found what he was looking for: the face of Dr. Martin Luther King.

He would have one chance.

Ray set the crosshairs over King's head.

He had aimed the 7-power Redfield telescopic sight at 6.5, which shrank the actual distance of 207.17 feet (just over the width of a football field) until it appeared to the shooter's eye to be just less than 32 feet. The telescopic sight made Ray into a better marksman than he actually was. King looked so close that Ray could almost see the pores in his skin.

It was 6:01 p.m., Central Standard Time. At the firehouse,

Patrolman W. B. Richmond kept his binoculars trained on the balcony. He told a fireman, George Loenneke, who was standing a few feet from him: "Dr. King is fixing to leave his hotel room." Loenneke said he had not seen King in two years and asked Richmond if he could take a look. The fireman peered through the peephole and saw King lean against the balcony.

In room 306, Ralph Abernathy faced the bathroom mirror and reached for a bottle of cologne. After he splashed some on, he would be ready to step outside, and he and Martin would walk along the balcony, go downstairs, and drive off to dinner.

James Earl Ray kept his right eye glued to the scope, and he kept King's face at the center of his field of vision.

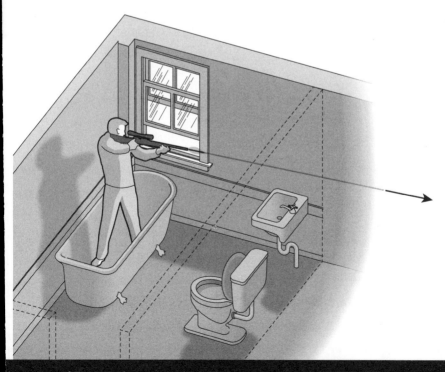

Illustration of Ray standing in the bathtub and shooting through the open window. Arrow indicates direction of the bullet.

From the firehouse, George Loenneke saw Dr. King turn slowly to his left, look down, and speak to people in the parking lot.

Ray kept King in his sights and squeezed the Gamemaster's trigger. The firing pin snapped forward and struck the rear of the chambered round.

The rifle responded with a loud crack and recoiled against Ray's right shoulder.

The barrel spit out a bullet at a speed of 2,670 feet per second, faster than the speed of sound or the echo of the shot.

A third of a second after Ray fired, the bullet struck King in the face, from above and from his right. It penetrated his right cheek, smashed through his jaw, and entered his neck. Then it angled down into the spinal column, passing through and damaging several vertebrae, severing his spine. Then the bullet took another weird, angled turn and came to rest in his left shoulder.

The force of the bullet lifted him up, pushing him backward and off his feet. It was as though an invisible heavyweight boxer had delivered a knockout punch to his opponent, and sent him sprawling onto the canvas. King landed on his back, faceup.

Then, a fraction of a second later, a violent, supersonic explosion disturbed the air.

Ralph Abernathy heard it through the open doorway to room 306: "I had sprinkled some Aramis cologne on my hands and was lifting them to my face when I heard a loud crack, and my hands jerked reflexively."

Abernathy thought that it sounded like the backfire of a car. But he had a bad feeling. The noise was louder and crisper than a misfiring automobile engine: "There was just enough difference to chill my heart."

At the firehouse, Patrolman Barney Wright from Tactical Unit 10 was relaxing in the lounge, sitting near a big picture window and reading a newspaper. He heard the plate-glass window rattle. Only a vibration or loud noise could do that. He looked up.

In the firehouse locker room, George Loenneke saw what had just happened. He turned to Patrolman Richmond and yelled: "Dr. King has been shot!" Then he ran to where the fire engines were parked and shouted the news. He burst into the lunchroom, where the other visiting policemen from Tactical Unit 10 were taking their break. They rushed out the door and ran toward the Lorraine Motel.

Ralph Abernathy reacted to the sound. "I wheeled, looked out the door, and saw only Martin's feet. He was down on the concrete balcony."

Abernathy ran outside and discovered his friend lying flat on his back, his legs tangled: "I bolted out the door and found him there, faceup, sprawled and unmoving."

He dropped to his knees and held King close: "I knelt down, gathered him in my arms, and began patting him on his left cheek . . . I could see that the bullet had entered his right cheek."

The two men gazed into each other's eyes: "I looked down at Martin's face. His eyes wobbled, then for an instant focused on me."

Abernathy tried to comfort him: "Martin. It's all right. Don't worry. This is Ralph. This is Ralph." He wanted his best friend to know that he would not die alone.

Abernathy saw that his friend could not speak: "His eyes grew calm and he moved his lips. I was certain he understood and was trying to say something. Then, in the next instant, I saw the understanding drain from his eyes and leave them absolutely empty." Martin Luther King, Jr., was dying. Abernathy saw the blood: "I looked more carefully at the wound and noticed the glistening blood and a flash of white bone."

Through his powerful telescopic sight, James Earl Ray must have seen the impact of the bullet and watched King fall. Ray withdrew the barrel from the window, stepped out of the tub, laid the rifle in the cardboard box, and wrapped the box in the blanket.

It was time to escape.

Ray opened the bathroom door and peered down the hallway. The coast was clear. He tucked the box under his arm, grabbed his little suitcase, and started walking. He did not want to leave the rifle behind. It would be a prized clue for the police. The rifle was stamped with a one-of-a-kind serial number. The manufacturer could trace it back to Aeromarine, the store that had sold it to the assassin. Yes, Ray had used a false name to buy it. But that would not prevent store employees from giving a physical description of him. And he had been to Aeromarine twice. Those visits had made an impression on the staff and on at least one customer, who had engaged him in conversation. Maybe this time, someone would remember too much about Ray.

Also, Ray might have left a careless fingerprint on the rifle or the cardboard box. He had been fingerprinted many times during his criminal career, and those were on file with various law enforcement agencies, including the FBI. Any prints he left behind now could

King's aides rushed to the balcony shortly after the shot was heard. They point in the direction the bullet came from. King lies in a pool of blood on the balcony.

Martin Luther King, Jr.'s view from his balcony, facing Ray's rooming house. The bathroom window from which Ray fired is circled.

be matched against existing police records. Eventually, they would reveal his true identity. It was better to take the risk of being seen carrying the murder weapon out of the rooming house than to leave it behind for the police.

Down in the parking lot of the Lorraine, it was a wild scene, with everyone shouting at once: "Dr. King has been shot!" "They killed him!" Several people even ducked behind cars for cover. Some of the men from Tactical Unit 10 made it from the firehouse to the Lorraine so fast that some of King's people thought they were under police attack. Others ran to the motel and rushed up the stairs to help Dr. King. He was still alive, but blood flowed from the wound, creating a widening puddle. One man pressed white cotton bath towels to his face, but they failed to stanch the bleeding.

There was so much blood.

James Earl Ray hoped to escape the rooming house without being seen by any of the other tenants. Several of them must have heard the shot, but had any of them opened their doors and come into the hallway to investigate? Ray would not find out until he opened the bathroom door and walked the length of the hallway. Several boarders *had* heard the rifle. Charlie Stephens opened his door as Ray hurried by and caught a glimpse of the assassin from behind. He did not see his face. Another one of the residents, Willie Anschutz, was already in the hall. Ray spotted him, looked down, and averted his eyes. He kept walking. Ray raised one of his hands and tried to cover his face.

"That sounded like a shot!" Anschutz said as Ray walked right by him.

"It *was*," Ray said as he rushed past.

Ray quickly approached the staircase landing and descended the nineteen steps. When he got to the first floor, he reached for the door that led to the sidewalk. Were the police already waiting outside, ready to capture him as he fled the building? There was only one way to find out. Ray opened the door. His eyes raced up and down South Main Street.

Ray looked south, to the left, at his white Mustang. It was parked only sixty feet away. He had to get to that car. It was urgent that he put as much distance between himself and the Lorraine Motel as he could. And then, he had to put as much distance as he could between himself and the city of Memphis.

The view of South Main Street, Memphis, Tennessee, looking south from Ray's rooming house. Ray exited the building and walked south to his waiting Mustang.

At the Lorraine, everyone—motel guests, employees, policemen, King's people—ran in the direction of the wounded victim. In the confusion, no one thought to fan out toward the nearby buildings that overlooked the Lorraine Motel parking lot and balconies. While stunned witnesses were still trying to figure out what had just happened, James Earl Ray left his rooming house.

However, once on South Main Street, just as Ray was about go to his car, toting his rifle under his arm, he noticed something that stopped him in his tracks. Two police cars and a police station wagon were parked in front of the firehouse at the end of the street. These were the cars of Tactical Unit 10. They spooked him. He didn't see any cops walking around on foot, but he thought that maybe they were in the cars.

Now he was afraid to carry the rifle to the Mustang. He made a spontaneous decision to abandon not only the weapon but also the suitcase in the recessed entry to the Canipe Amusement Company, next door to the rooming house. Ray got rid of the bag and the rifle—still wrapped in the box and the blanket—by tossing them against the door. From Canipe's, less than sixty feet stood between Ray and his escape car.

Canipe's was closed for the evening, but the owner, who was working late inside, heard a thud at his front door. He caught a glimpse of Ray through the window and went to investigate. Canipe found the blanket-wrapped bundle and the bag at his doorstep. By the time he stepped outside, Ray was gone.

But Canipe noticed a white Mustang pulling away from the curb fast.

Ray abandoned his suitcase and rifle in the entry of the Canipe Amusement Company between the rooming house and his Mustang, parked a short distance away.

Less than five minutes after he had assassinated Martin Luther King, James Earl Ray had escaped the scene of the crime. He was gone even before the ambulance arrived, and before any policemen arrived on South Main Street to seal off the exits from the rooming house and the other buildings nearby.

While King's crumpled body still lay on the balcony of the Lorraine Motel, Ray drove his white Mustang into the fast-approaching twilight and vanished into the night.

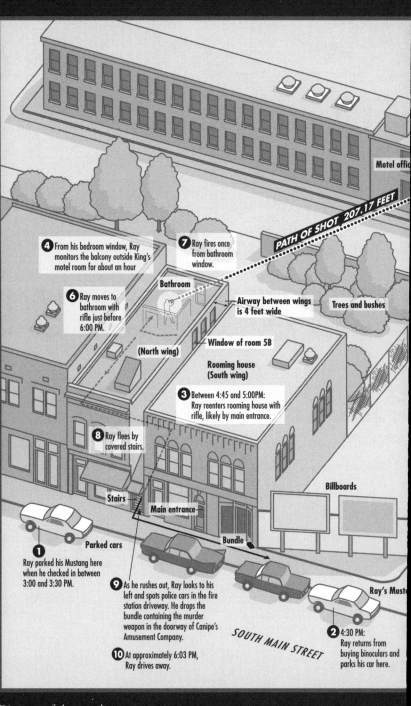

Diagram of the murder scene.

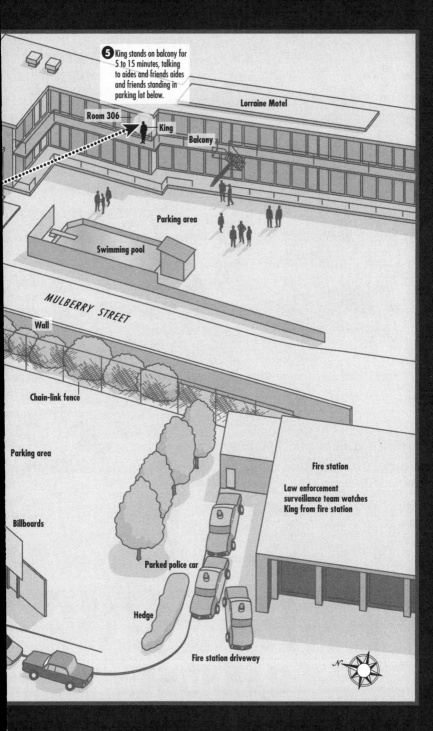

PART FOUR
MANHUNT!

ESCAPING MEMPHIS

With only a minute or two to spare, James Earl Ray had fled the scene before the first police report even hit the airwaves.

After Patrolman Barney Wright had heard the firehouse window rattle, he ran outside to the retaining wall that stood between him and the Lorraine Motel. People at the Lorraine shouted across the parking lot that King had been shot. Wright ran back to one of the police cars parked in the firehouse driveway, while Patrolman E. E. Douglas jumped into the seat next to him and got on the radio.

At 6:03 p.m., Tactical Unit 10, at the firehouse, radioed the news to a police dispatcher: "We have information that King was shot at the Lorraine."

Dispatch: "Repeat your information again, Tact. 10."

Tact. 10: "We have information that King was shot at the Lorraine."

The dispatcher alerted other police cars: "Tact. 9 and Tact. 8, pull into the Lorraine, report of a shooting . . . any cruisers on the air in the vicinity of the Lorraine, 406 Mulberry?"

Tact. 18 replied: "We are close by, we are on that."

6:04 p.m. Dispatch: "Okay, Tact. 18, any other cars in the area?"

Two other police cars called in to say that they were already arriving on the scene. The dispatcher, concerned that the call from Tactical Unit 10 might be a false alarm, radioed instructions to all cars converging on the scene.

Dispatch: "All cars on the Lorraine Hotel call . . . all men are to remain in the cars until it has been verified."

Instantly, Tactical 10, the first unit to report the shooting, cut in at 6:04 p.m. to confirm the news: "He has been shot."

At 6:05 p.m., dispatch ordered all police cars in the area to converge on the scene: "All tact. units on the call, you are to form a ring around the Lorraine Hotel. You are to form a ring around the Lorraine Hotel. No one is to enter or leave. No traffic, no pedestrian traffic, is to enter or leave the area at the Lorraine Hotel. A ring is to be formed around the hotel as soon as possible."

Any policeman who heard that call might have assumed that King had been shot from close range by someone at the Lorraine. Within seconds, one police car after another got on the radio and raced there: "In the area." "In area." "On scene." "On the scene." "We're in the loop, put us on that call."

At 6:06 p.m., dispatch gave more details: "We have information that the shot came from a brick building directly east—correction—directly west from Lorraine."

The report was a few minutes too late.

The dispatcher added more details: "Tact. 10 has information that he was shot from a brick building directly across from the Lorraine . . .

the circle is to include the building west of the Lorraine. The brick building from where the shot was fired . . . all units . . . seal this area off completely . . . seal off this area completely."

By now, James Earl Ray was already beyond the tight perimeter that the police were forming around the building.

But the assassin had left behind a treasure trove of evidence. Mr. Canipe called out to a police detective who had just walked onto Main Street and showed him the bundle in his vestibule. The detective reported his find over the radio.

At 6:07 p.m., Tactical Unit 10 broke in with urgent news: "I have the weapon in front of 424 and the subject ran south on Main Street."

Then the dispatcher broke the news that Canipe had reported: ". . . the subject responsible for the shooting is running south on Main Street. [Tact. 10] has the weapon at 424 Main, and the subject ran south from that location." Several police cars headed to the scene.

6:07 p.m. dispatch broadcast instructions: "Not to touch the weapon. The weapon is not to be touched." It was vital to preserve any fingerprints of the shooter. Careless handling might smear the prints and ruin the evidence. "Repeating . . . the subject ran south on Main . . . any physical description of the subject?"

Tact. 10: "All we know is he is a young white male, well dressed, dark colored suit . . ." The rest was inaudible.

6:08 p.m. "He's a young white male, well dressed, a young white male well dressed, ran south from 424 South Main."

James Earl Ray, as he appeared in April 1968, dressed in a dark suit, wearing horn-rimmed glasses.

At 6:10 p.m., nine minutes since the shooting, Tactical Unit 10 reported another important clue: "It's also believed that this subject left in a late model white Mustang, going north on Main."

Dispatch repeated the information at once: "Information that subject may be in a late model white Mustang, a late model white Mustang, north on Main Street. A white Mustang . . . a young white male, well dressed, possibly in a late model white Mustang, went north on Main." Dispatch repeated the information two minutes later.

Ten minutes after the shooting, an ambulance pulled into the Lorraine Motel parking lot.

TO THE HOSPITAL

In 1968, ambulances were more primitive than they are today, being little more than station wagons that transported sick or injured people. They carried no medical equipment and no paramedics rode aboard them to begin lifesaving treatment at the scene. Indeed, in those days, many ambulances did double duty as hearses. Martin Luther King would have to wait until he got to the hospital to receive proper medical treatment.

While King was sped ahead to the hospital, Ray continued his escape. By 6:10 p.m., dispatch announced that King was en route: "Ambulance on the way."

Car 315 interjected: "Patrolman Wolfe is in the fire department ambulance with him."

Dispatch: "Okay, the fire department ambulance has cleared the scene . . . all tactical units are to pull into the area, all tactical units are to pull into the area."

At 6:13 p.m., Detective R. R. Davis and Lieutenant T. H. Smith arrived at the Lorraine parking lot and tried to interview eyewitnesses who had congregated in the courtyard below King's balcony. Several people refused to make a statement.

James Bevel from the Southern Christian Leadership Conference was angry and would not speak to the investigators. Detectives Davis and Smith got little help: "Some of these people walked away from us . . . we attempted to interview others, but they either had no comment, or indicated that they were angry or grief stricken and did not feel up to talking."

Many more of King's associates were also uncooperative. That was understandable. Civil rights activists had suffered years of police harassment. In many cases, racist sheriffs had stood by or even participated in violence against blacks. It was natural for King's comrades to be suspicious of law enforcement. Ben Branch said he did not want to talk. "He seemed," according to the policemen, "to be in a very angry mood, and was very hostile towards the investigating officers." They tried a second time. Branch walked away again. On their third attempt to interview him, Branch told them he was standing in the parking lot directly beneath King, who was on the balcony. He heard a shot, and King fell. Branch did not know where the shot came from and saw no one fleeing the immediate area. "He did state that he saw several police officers across Mulberry Street, behind the bushes, and it looked kind of funny to him that they could have gotten up there so fast." Branch implied that the police must have had something to do with the assassination.

Reverand Billy Kyles said he had just come out of room 306 with King and was talking to him on the balcony. He said he parted with King and was walking along the balcony toward the stairway, when he heard a shot, turned, and saw that Dr. King had fallen.

Jesse Jackson was standing in the courtyard when it happened. He was looking up at King and did not see where the shot came from. He, too, said that he could not understand how the police got there so fast.

The ambulance ride took just four minutes. At 6:14 p.m. it arrived at the hospital—only thirteen minutes after the shooting. The treatment report described King's appearance when he was wheeled into emergency room number 1: "The patient [was] totally unconscious and flat on his back . . . There was a large gaping wound in the root of the neck which was not actively bleeding at the time of his initial arrival. There was much blood on his clothes, neck, and shoulder."

A doctor grabbed a stethoscope and detected a palpable heartbeat and radial pulse. Somehow, King was still alive. The doctor ordered two cutdowns immediately. It was a procedure to insert tubes into two veins, in order to give King necessary fluids, and to infuse blood into him under pressure, to replace what he had lost. A surgeon performed a tracheotomy and inserted a breathing tube into the throat, which provided essential oxygen. King's heartbeat was weak, so the doctors tried to resuscitate it by injecting it with adrenaline and performing closed-chest cardiac massage.

These surgeons tried desperately to save Martin Luther King, Jr.'s life. They discovered that on his right side, the bullet had severed his jugular vein and had shredded an artery, which protruded from the wound. One of his lungs was filling with blood. Surgeons clamped the blood vessels and inserted a chest tube to drain blood from King's right chest and re-inflate his lung. The tube immediately drained 1,000 cc of blood from his chest. That's over four cups, or about 20 percent, of his body's fluid. The doctors also discovered that the bullet had damaged part of his spine; they detected a serious loss of spinal fluid. The pupils of King's eyes were now fixed and massively dilated; they showed no reaction to light.

At 6:16 p.m., dispatch radioed an order to keep reporters away from the Lorraine: "all newsmen to be withheld from the area." And then Dispatch rebroadcast all available information about the suspect: "Repeating the information at this time, the weapon was dropped at 424 South Main, a well-dressed young white male, last seen running south from that location, may be in a late model white Mustang, north on Main."

So many police cars were using their radios simultaneously that dispatch could not hear their reports: "Cut off some of the radios at the Lorraine, we're getting too much feedback. Cut off some of the radios."

Now Tactical Unit 10 could get through with additional, important details: "Subject had dark hair, possibly black, the suit was a very dark suit, also possibly black, and the subject was medium heavy build." But this could have been a description of just about anyone.

At 6:20 p.m., car 150 reported on King's status: "The hospital advised critical condition."

At 6:34 p.m., car 421 reported a lead: "We're stopping a white Mustang, north on Thomas from Firestone, with a white male in it." "We've stopped that car, and he checks out okay." "Was he able to furnish any information?" No. Just to be sure, they held the driver. "Transporting to headquarters."

It was a false alarm. It was not James Earl Ray.

A HOT TIP AND A HOAX

After several white Mustang sightings turned out to be erroneous, a hot tip went out over the radio that, for the next thirteen minutes, mesmerized every policeman who heard it.

At 6:35, dispatch announced breaking news: "160 has information from a complainant that a white male is east on Summer from Highland, a white male east on Summer from Highland in a white Mustang, in a white Mustang responsible for this shooting . . . subject is exceeding the speed limit."

160: "This car is speeding over 65 miles per hour."

Dispatch: "Advising that this car is speeding 75 miles per hour north on Mendenhall from Summer."

The details got more incredible by the minute.

Dispatch: "Advising approximately . . . 100 miles per hour."

160: "This white Mustang is shooting at the blue Pontiac following him."

Excited by the chase, the dispatcher made a mistake.

Dispatch: "Advising that the blue Pontiac is shooting at the white

Mustang . . . the subject is firing at the white Mustang . . . the Mustang is a citizen's band unit."

160: "Correction on that, the Mustang is shooting at the Pontiac."

Dispatch: "All cars correction, 160 is advising that the white Mustang, this is a white Mustang that is firing at the blue Pontiac, approaching the Millington Road that goes to the naval base."

But this turned out to be a hoax. It started when an anonymous citizen reported that he had just spotted the white Mustang headed out of Memphis. The tipster claimed he had an amateur CB radio in his car, and that he was following the Mustang. He began to broadcast a play-by-play of the pursuit. The reports became more dramatic by the minute. According to the tipster, when the driver of the Mustang noticed that he was being followed, he sped away. The voice on the radio said he was now pursuing the suspect in a high-speed chase, so police dispatchers directed police cars to the coordinates that the voice on the radio gave them. Then, suddenly, the voice shouted over the radio that the Mustang had crashed and that the driver had opened fire on him with a pistol.

The broadcast should have aroused suspicion. First, the anonymous person who contacted the police by radio claimed that he saw three white males in the Mustang, while eyewitnesses at the crime scene had reported only one. Second, the tipster, who never identified himself, also said that he could not close the distance to the Mustang to read its license plate number because one of its occupants had opened fire on him and one of the gunshots had shattered his windshield. However, the police, desperate to catch King's killer, were tricked by the faulty information.

In retrospect, it is clear that there was not enough time for the tipster to have driven the distances he was claiming. In addition, the radio signal was too strong and did not weaken as he drove farther away, suggesting that he was actually sitting still in one location rather than in a moving car. Police patrol cars that raced to intercept the Mustang and its pursuer failed to find those vehicles anywhere on the road along their alleged route. And finally, no other witnesses had called the police to report a high-speed chase and shots fired.

The radio broadcast was a fake. It had sent the Memphis police on a wild-goose chase from 6:35 to 6:49 p.m. In the critical minutes after James Earl Ray's escape, the voice had diverted police manpower from setting up patrols and roadblocks that might have led to Ray's capture. Detectives speculated that the assassin had a co-conspirator who timed the radio broadcast to throw them off the trail and help the killer escape Memphis. The broadcast accomplished that, but if Ray had an accomplice, it was not this person. Later, an investigation revealed that the perpetrator of this hoax was a malicious teenager who was playing what he thought was a funny prank. He had no connection to Ray or the assassination.

Back at the South Main Street rooming house, detectives searched Ray's room. They found little evidence—a thirty-seven-inch black plastic carrying strap for the binoculars, a dark green pillow, and a few burned matches. In the bathroom, they looked in the bottom of the tub and saw several dirty smears, as though someone had been standing there in his shoes. On the wall they found a handprint, as though someone had steadied himself while stepping into the tub.

At the emergency room at St. Joseph's Hospital, additional surgeons had arrived to treat King. An electrocardiogram (EKG) showed no heart function. For fifty minutes the doctors continued cardiac massage and other resuscitation methods to try to restore King's pulse and heart function.

King had been lucky once before. Ten years ago, when he had almost been stabbed through the heart, the doctors had been able to save his life. But nothing was working now. King was showing no response or any kind of vital signs. The life force had drained out of him.

Approximately one hour after the assassination, the doctors knew they could do no more.

It was over.

At 7:05 p.m., Central Standard Time, Dr. Jerome Barrasso pronounced Martin Luther King, Jr., dead. He was only thirty-nine years old.

However, Dr. King's journey was not yet over. He would make two more trips tonight: first to the morgue, and then to a funeral home. At the morgue, Dr. Jerry Francisco, the Shelby County medical examiner, photographed the fatal bullet and the wounds that it inflicted. The autopsy recited the emotionless facts and numbers of death: King's height and weight; the measure of his internal organs on a scientific scale; even the mass of his brain, which just a few hours ago had been the source of his courage, compassion, and conviction, all the qualities that made King the remarkable man he was. Then there was the list of King's personal effects: "Shirt, Necktie, Suit Coat, Trousers, Pair of Socks, Undershorts, Undershirt, Pair of Shoes, three $20 bills," and the contents of his pockets.

When the autopsy was finished, the same white car that had picked King up yesterday at the airport and chauffeured him around Memphis for the past two days now went to pick up his body. Ralph

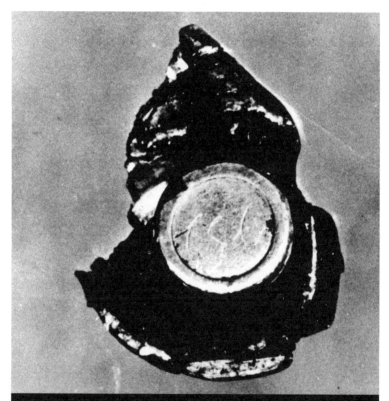

The bullet that killed Martin Luther King, Jr., removed from his body during the autopsy. A rear-end view of the bullet shows how badly it was deformed on impact.

Abernathy accompanied his old friend's body to a funeral home. The morticians would have a lot of work to do to conceal the gaping wound to King's face, and Abernathy wanted to make sure they did it right.

Miles away, James Earl Ray drove on in the night, using dark side roads to avoid being spotted. As he approached the Tennessee state line, no police roadblocks barred his route, so he crossed into Mississippi. Ray must have listened to news flashes on his car radio, but the early, sketchy reports said only that Martin Luther King had been shot and wounded. Later reports gave more details, until at last Ray heard the news he had been waiting for.

Martin Luther King, Jr., was dead. And his killer was on the loose.

"Leaving Memphis I had to drive slow and be careful so as to not attract attention and get arrested for speeding. I drove south into Mississippi for a while, then turned east across Mississippi and Alabama, through Birmingham to Atlanta," Ray said. "But nobody stopped me."

For the time being, he was safe. He possessed certain advantages. No one knew the assassin's name—the police had no idea of his true identity. He had used two different false names to buy the rifle and register at the South Main Street rooming house. He had left nothing behind in his room that bore his real name, and the police did not possess the license plate number of his car. No one in Memphis had any photographs of him. And Aeromarine, where he had bought the rifle, did not have surveillance cameras. At this moment, no one in the world was hunting for a man named James Earl Ray, or suspected that he had just murdered Dr. King. Ray needed to go into deep hiding before the authorities could discover who he was.

Ray was heading to a strange destination—Atlanta, King's hometown. Somewhere during the eleven-hour drive between Memphis and his next stop, Ray tossed out of the window of the moving car the few possessions he had in the vehicle, mostly camera equipment. He planned to return to his Atlanta rooming house. He wanted to catch his breath, regroup, and then embark on the second stage of his escape. Ray's journey had led him to seek refuge within a few miles of King's grieving widow.

AFTERMATH AT THE MOTEL AND ACROSS THE NATION

King's entourage returned to the Lorraine Motel and gathered in room 306. Martin's blood still stained the concrete walkway outside the door. To enter the room, his friends had to step over a pool of the dark liquid that was more than three feet long.

Inside, King's friends and followers talked. They mourned. It was real. The unthinkable had finally happened. They always feared, as did King, that this day would come. King's briefcase still lay open, as if he had just stepped out and expected to return. It contained his shaving kit, various personal items, and a copy of one of his books.

King's entourage meets in his motel room after the assassination. King's blood was still wet on the concrete outside the room.

Upon the death of King, the mantle of leadership passed wordlessly to his friend, spiritual brother, and logical heir, Ralph Abernathy. No vote of King's aides was needed and none was taken. A news photographer who was present captured the melancholy scene of King's men sitting around the room.

The photographer captured more gruesome images on the balcony. One depicts Theatrice Bailey, the motel owner's brother, trying to sweep away a large puddle of blood with a bristle dust broom. Another shows him, knees bent, crouching low to the ground, using a painter's spatula to scoop up coagulated blood and gore and

Theatrice Bailey sweeps up Martin Luther King's blood from the balcony outside room 306.

Bailey scoops King's blood into a jar.

175

deposit it in a clear glass jar. Later, the stained concrete had to be washed down with soap and water. But the jar and its contents, like a holy relic of a saint, were preserved. For years, the morbid souvenir languished on the back shelf of a home refrigerator.

In Washington, DC, the news reached President Lyndon Johnson at the White House. He was horrified. Yes, he and Martin Luther King had disagreed about the Vietnam War, and Johnson believed that King had betrayed him. But they had once been close and had embraced each other as partners in the civil rights cause. Immediately, LBJ canceled an out-of-town trip. He turned on the several television sets that he kept in the Oval Office to watch simultaneous news broadcasts on the three major networks. King's brutal murder crushed LBJ. He knew what a disaster for America it would be. It turned out to be worse than he could have imagined.

As news of the assassination spread across the land on the night of April 4, no one knew what would happen next. When darkness fell across the American continent, the nation became a tinderbox. The murder of Dr. King unleashed a spasm of anger, resentment, vandalism, looting, arson, and gunfire, all of the things that Martin Luther King had tried for a decade to prevent. His murder caused an American upheaval.

In the tragic aftermath of the assassination, many people mourned. But some took to the streets, driven by feelings of helplessness and rage. The death of the great civil rights leader shook the nation and unleashed powerful forces. Riots broke out in more than one hundred cities. Dozens of people were killed, and hundreds injured.

In Chicago, fires rage in the rioting in the aftermath of the King assassination.

Only storefronts remain standing in this Washington, DC, street after riots

Sections of Los Angeles; Chicago; and Washington, DC, went up in flames. In Chicago alone, three hundred square blocks were partially or fully consumed by fire. Thousands of businesses were destroyed. The National Guard was called out to protect the U.S. Capitol from attack. And the assassin had vanished from the scene of the crime, leaving behind his rifle—but no answers as to why he had done it. African Americans blamed a racist society for King's death, and the social unrest that followed in its wake threatened to undermine all the progress that King's work had achieved.

In Washington, DC, federal troops guard the United States Capitol when rioting breaks out following the King assassination.

On the night of King's assassination, Senator Robert F. Kennedy (brother of slain president John F. Kennedy) was in Indianapolis, Indiana, campaigning for the 1968 Democratic presidential nomination. Before boarding a plane for the city, he was told that King had been shot and wounded. When he landed, Kennedy learned that King had already died. The senator did not want to cancel his appearance, so he made his way to Seventeenth and Broadway, a poor section of town where he would speak to a black audience. When Kennedy arrived, it was obvious that the crowd hadn't heard the news yet. They did not know that Martin Luther King was dead.

He asked supporters holding signs to lower them so that everyone could see him.

Kennedy began to speak.

"I have some very sad news for all of you, and, I think, sad news for all our fellow citizens, and people who love peace all over the world."

No one knew what he was going to say next: "Martin Luther King was shot and killed tonight in Memphis, Tennessee."

Gasps and moans arose from the crowd. Some people shouted "No!"

Kennedy continued:

> "Martin Luther King dedicated his life to love and to justice between fellow human beings. He died in the cause of that effort. In this difficult day, in this difficult time for the United States, it's perhaps well to ask what kind of a

nation we are and what direction we want to move in. For those of you who are black—considering the evidence that there were white people who were responsible—you can be filled with bitterness, and with hatred, and a desire for revenge."

Kennedy pleaded with them to remain peaceful:

"We can move in that direction as a country, in greater polarization—black people amongst blacks, and whites amongst whites, filled with hatred toward one another. Or we can make an effort, as Martin Luther King did, to understand, and to comprehend, and replace that violence, that stain of bloodshed that has spread across our land, with an effort to understand, compassion, and love.

"For those of you who are black and are tempted to . . . be filled with hatred and mistrust of the injustice of such an act, against all white people, I would only say that I can also feel in my own heart the same kind of feeling."

Robert Kennedy had never before spoken in public about the assassination of his brother, President John F. Kennedy. It had so seared his soul that he could not bear to discuss it. Now, on this extraordinary night, he broke his rule: "I had a member of my family killed, but he was killed by a white man."

enator Robert F. Kennedy, on the presidential primary campaign trail, addresses a
owd in Indianapolis, Indiana. He informed those gathered that Martin Luther King
d been assassinated.

Kennedy asked the audience not to give in to despair and cynicism:

> "What we need in the United States is not division; what we need in the United States is not hatred; what we need in the United States is not violence and lawlessness, but is love, and wisdom, and compassion toward one another, [and a] feeling of justice toward those who still suffer within our country, whether they be white or whether they be black.

Kennedy closed with a plea for peace:

> "[Let us] dedicate ourselves to what the Greeks wrote so many years ago: to tame the savageness of man and make gentle the life of this world. Let us dedicate ourselves to that, and say a prayer for our country and for our people."

This speech would be remembered as the finest one that Robert Kennedy ever gave. There was no riot in Indianapolis that night. But as Kennedy begged for peace in that city, riots in other places were breaking out in the streets of urban America.

It is possible that Robert Kennedy felt some remorse or even guilt that night. He was aware that the FBI director J. Edgar Hoover had wiretapped and hounded Martin Luther King. But Hoover alone

President John F. Kennedy with FBI Director J. Edgar Hoover and Attorney General Robert Kennedy.

did not have the legal power to spy on him. He needed authorization from his boss, the attorney general of the United States. And it was then-Attorney General Robert Kennedy who had signed the order allowing Hoover to conduct the surveillance. But that information was not public knowledge.

And what of the man who had ordered the campaign of wiretapping, surveillance, and harassment against Martin Luther King? FBI director J. Edgar Hoover was an American legend. He had been in power for decades, and he ruled the FBI with an iron fist. Few leaders dared challenge him. It was rumored that he had collected secret files on most of the important figures in public life, especially politicians, and even presidents. He judged King harshly. In Hoover's secret 1964 letter to his deputy, William Sullivan, he had written that King's "exposure is long overdue" and he hoped that the civil rights leader was about to get his "just deserts." Now, four years later, King had suffered even more than Hoover had hoped.

Hoover assumed that he was done with Martin Luther King and could close his files on him. He was wrong. Yes, it was true that King's murder was not a federal matter. It was a local crime. The assassin had violated the homicide laws of the state of Tennessee. Memphis police and state authorities had jurisdiction over the case. But President Lyndon Johnson and Attorney General Ramsey Clark had other ideas. They knew that there would be a national uproar if this investigation were left in the hands of local authorities. Martin Luther King was one of the most famous men in the world. The American people would demand that the nation's premier law enforcement agency lead the investigation. It was decided that night. Attorney General Clark ordered J. Edgar Hoover—one of King's harshest enemies—to take charge of the manhunt to track down his killer.

Hoover was astute enough to know that he could not allow his personal hatred of King to impede the investigation. This would turn out to be the most important investigation in the history of the FBI. Hoover knew it was essential that his special agents identify and capture King's murderer. In the days ahead, Hoover employed every asset at his disposal and held nothing back to investigate the murder of the very man he had harassed and despised. Hoover placed the bureau's assistant director, Cartha "Deke" DeLoach, in charge of the matter. Hoover's orders were clear: The FBI must not fail. No one—not Hoover, Attorney General Clark, or President Johnson—realized yet what a difficult assignment this would prove to be.

Ralph Abernathy spent the night of April 4 alone in room 306. King's empty bed stood nearby. The death of Martin Luther King was a tragedy for African Americans, for the civil rights movement, and for the whole nation. But it was also a deep personal loss for his best friend, Ralph Abernathy. They had been inseparable brothers-in-arms in the fight for civil rights, and had known each other for seventeen years, since 1951.

The Lorraine Motel lights burn brightly against a dark sky.

Mourners placed memorial wreaths and signs outside room 306 at the Lorraine Motel following King's assassination.

Abernathy did not mourn alone. Somebody hung a solitary wreath of flowers on the motel room door. Then another one appeared. And another. Soon, dozens of wreaths and floral arrangements from anonymous mourners framed the doorway and hung from the balcony railing.

THE FBI INVESTIGATION

On the morning of April 5, at around 5:00 a.m., the evidence that the FBI had collected in Memphis arrived in Washington, DC, for investigation and forensic analysis. Attorney General Ramsey Clark and FBI assistant director Deke DeLoach flew to Memphis early that morning to show how seriously the federal government was taking the case.

Later that morning, an FBI agent went to the Aeromarine store, where the owner's son verified that they had sold the murder weapon, as confirmed by the gun's serial number: 461,476. He could give only a vague description of the buyer, even though the purchaser had come back a second time to buy a more powerful rifle.

When the FBI interviewed another customer who had spoken to Ray, they got a better description, including insights into whether the assassin had knowledge of firearms or was an experienced hunter. The customer said he doubted it. The FBI agent in charge in Memphis, Robert Jensen, handled the initial investigation and supervised the collection of the first pieces of evidence.

Ray left behind a potential treasure trove in front of Canipe's store. From this location, officials had retrieved the Remington Gamemaster rifle and the Redfield scope in a cardboard rifle box, which were wrapped in a blanket. Here they also found the cheap blue suitcase measuring twenty by thirty inches, containing maps, newspapers, the binoculars, some clothing, a tube of toothpaste, a can of shaving cream, a transistor radio, two cans of beer, and a twenty-round cardboard ammunition box containing nine cartridges. From the bathroom of the rooming house, they recovered one spent brass bullet casing, while in the bedroom, they only found the carrying strap for the binoculars.

All of this material was processed, labeled, and bagged to document the chain of custody before it was rushed to FBI headquarters in Washington. The bureau collected other evidence, too: the mangled bullet that was excised from King's body at the autopsy, as well as King's bloody clothes. Agents even removed the windowsill from the rooming house bathroom window.

The same morning, April 5, at around 6:00 a.m., James Earl Ray arrived in Atlanta.

And that morning in cities scattered all across America, the rising sun revealed plumes of smoke ascending from the ruins of burned buildings. Americans awoke to newspaper headlines of nationwide looting, arson, violence, and murder.

Ray did not plan to remain in Atlanta for long. He retrieved his .38-caliber revolver from his room and dropped off some clothes for cleaning at the local laundry, probably to create a false impression

The day after the assassination, civil rights leader and King friend Jesse Jackson reads newspaper coverage of the murder.

In Memphis and across the country, grieving citizens displayed handmade signs and banners mourning the murder of Dr. King.

that he had not left town. He also left a misleading note for his landlord, indicating that he would return sometime in the future. Of course he gave false information—it was just a ruse in case the police ever came calling for him. He might have bought a copy of the newspaper to read about his crime.

Ray would have to part ways with his beloved Mustang. He loved the car, and it had served him well on several important journeys, including the cross-country drive from California to Memphis, and during his escape from Memphis to Atlanta after the assassination. But the word was out. The police were looking for a well-dressed white man driving a late-model, light-colored Mustang. He had another long journey ahead of him, but it was too risky to keep it. Ray had to ditch it.

Ray drove his car into the parking lot of the Capitol Homes public housing. He wiped it down to smear any identifiable fingerprints, then he abandoned it there. He proceeded to the Greyhound station and caught a bus out of town. He had a long way to go. His first destination was Cincinnati, Ohio.

While Ray rode the highways, the FBI was on the case. As soon as the initial evidence arrived in Washington, the agency's legendary fingerprint lab went to work. Meticulous technicians examined every item with intense scrutiny. As a career criminal, Ray knew all about fingerprint evidence, a knowledge he demonstrated when he tried to wipe down the Mustang. But he had been in a hurry in room 5B and in the bathroom; thus, when he fled the rooming house after he shot King, it was possible that he accidentally left some prints there. He might have also left prints on his rifle or on the items in his suitcase. It was the lab's job to find out if he did. Without fingerprints, it would be much harder for the FBI to identify the assassin.

The lab announced its results—it had pulled six fingerprints. They came from the rifle, the scope, the binoculars, a newspaper, a bottle of aftershave, and a beer can. It was the first major break in the case. Now the Bureau had to identify to whom these prints belonged.

The FBI firearms lab went to work trying to match the bullet recovered from King's body to the suspected murder weapon, Ray's rifle. Once fired from a weapon, a bullet has a unique set of markings on it. Agents of the FBI can fire a bullet from a gun and use a microscope to compare the rifling grooves on the test bullet to the bullet recovered from the victim's body. Bureau agents conducted ballistic tests to determine whether the bullet recovered from King's body could have been fired from the rifle found in the recessed entry of Canipe's on South Main Street. They concluded that the bullet extracted from King's body was fired from the same type of barrel as the rifle found on Main Street, and that the fatal bullet was of the same type of unfired rounds discovered at the rooming house. The bullet *could* have been fired from the Gamemaster, but its passage through King's body had left it too damaged to allow the lab to match any marks on it to the rifling pattern of the barrel.

———————

"Nobody paid any attention to me on the bus or at the bus stops," Ray recalled. So when his first bus arrived in Cincinnati at 1:30 a.m. on April 6, he then took another north to Detroit, Michigan. He was making a break for the Canadian border. He arrived in Detroit at 8:00 a.m. and took a taxi to Windsor, Canada. It was as simple as that. James Earl Ray had escaped the United States. At noon on April 6, he took a four-hour train ride to Toronto. The next morning, Palm Sunday, Ray watched the news on television. The identity of King's assassin was still unknown.

Ray was determined to keep it that way and began work on an ingenious scheme. "On Monday [April 8] I went to the library and went through birth announcements for 1932," he recalled. Ray asked to see old newspapers from October and November, 1932.

What did he hope to find?

"I was looking for two names to use in applying for a passport," and he wrote down ten possibilities, including birth dates, names of parents, and mothers' maiden names. Though he had been born in 1928, he thought he could pass for younger, possibly due to his plastic surgery.

Then he cross-referenced those names with the current Toronto telephone directory, where he found two of them, including a man named Ramon George Sneyd.

He then called Sneyd on the telephone.

"Posing as a government employee, I telephoned . . . [him] to see if [he] had ever had a passport. I couldn't use the name of anyone who had ever had a passport as his picture would be on file."

The answer was no. Ray had his new identity.

Ray did not want to stay in Canada forever. He wanted to escape to another country, but for that he needed a passport—and one not in his own name.

But here Ray made a critical mistake. He immediately got photos taken but failed to apply for a passport right away. He did not realize how easy it was to get a Canadian passport and mistakenly thought he would also need a documented birth certificate in order to prove his new identity—that of George Sneyd. For this, he would need to request a duplicate copy from a government office—which he did, posing as Sneyd. But such requests take time, and this left Ray waiting aimlessly, allowing the FBI to close in.

The FBI suspected that the assassin had spent the night prior to the murder somewhere in or near Memphis, but they had no clue where. Per its famous strategy of canvassing, the Bureau deployed agents in a systematic grid. Agents began visiting all the hotels, motels, and rooming houses in the area, hoping that the assassin had stayed at one of them. At the New Rebel Motel, they hit the jackpot and discovered that a man using the name Eric S. Galt, claiming to be an Alabama resident, had checked out on April 4. He had driven a white Mustang with Alabama license plates 1-38993. The FBI obtained copies of the car registration and tracked down the original owner, who had sold it to Ray, who had bought it under a false name. But where was the car? It was still sitting in the parking lot of the Capitol Homes apartments in Atlanta! The Mustang had attracted the attention of residents, who speculated whether it was the one wanted in the assassination. On April 10, a tenant finally reported the car to the police, but authorities were slow to respond. Finally, on April 11, the FBI seized the car and all the possessions

James Earl Ray's abandoned Mustang, in the parking lot of a housing complex.

that Ray had left in it. One of the most valuable clues was an oil change sticker from a car dealership in California.

The evidence pointed to a man named Eric Starvo Galt, who had at one time lived in California. The investigation shifted to the West Coast. From laundry tickets, the FBI learned Galt's California address, and that he had left a forwarding order to have all his mail sent on for general delivery at the main post office in Atlanta. Now this evidence connected both East and West Coasts. Was Galt the same man who used the John Willard name to register at the

Memphis rooming house across from the Lorraine Motel on April 4? And was Galt the man who had used the name Lowmeyer to buy the Gamemaster rifle from the Aeromarine store?

Were Galt, Willard, and Lowmeyer all the same man?

And was this man—whoever he was—the murderer of Dr. King?

While the FBI intensified its pursuit of the still unidentified assassin, Martin Luther King, Jr.'s family and the nation prepared to bid King farewell.

Several days earlier, on Friday, April 5, the day after the assassination, Coretta Scott King had flown to Memphis. There she claimed her husband's body so he could be buried at home in Atlanta. When the plane landed, she had their children brought aboard. She wanted them to see their father now, in private, before the public viewing later.

But the children were confused. "Mommy, where's Daddy?" their five-year-old daughter, Bernice, asked, puzzled that her father was not there waiting for her.

Coretta struggled to make her understand. "Daddy is lying down in his casket in the back of the plane," she said, "When you see him, he won't be able to speak to you." The good-byes had to be heartbreakingly one-sided, because, as their mother explained, "Daddy has gone to live with God, and he won't be coming back."

Mourners, overcome by emotion, file by the open casket of Martin Luther King, Jr., to pay their last respects.

The next day, on the afternoon of Saturday, April 6, King's body was driven from the Hanley's Bell Street Funeral Home, where it had lain in repose overnight, to Sisters Chapel at Spelman College, one of the prominent, historically black colleges in the South. Because the morticians had repaired and concealed the major damage to his face, Coretta agreed to allow a public viewing.

Over the next two days, sixty thousand people came to say their good-byes. Long lines formed on the campus, at one point extending

over a mile. News photographers captured the grief as mourners filed past their dead hero. One heartbreaking image depicted Coretta and the children gazing upon the slain husband and father.

Dr. King had warned in his last speech that he might not get to the Promised Land, and now his prophecy had come true. On Sunday, April 7, in churches all across America, ministers led their congregations in prayers, seeking comfort for a grieving nation. That day was even proclaimed a national day of mourning by President Lyndon B. Johnson.

Coretta Scott King and her children gaze on Martin Luther King's body in an open casket.

Even though he was gone, Dr. King's dreams were not. On April 8, Coretta Scott King flew back to Memphis to carry on her husband's legacy. Before his death, Martin Luther King, Jr., had pledged to lead a march of the striking sanitation workers and their supporters. Now, in his absence, she and others, such as Ralph Abernathy, entertainer Harry Belafonte, and her three eldest children, led the procession of twenty thousand people. After this stirring tribute, Coretta and the group flew back to Atlanta that same day.

On the evening of April 8, King's body was moved from Spelman College to Ebenezer Baptist Church in preparation for the funeral the next day and the final farewell to the great leader. Massive crowds lined the streets and surrounded the church. From all over the nation, civil rights leaders, movie stars, and political leaders had converged on Atlanta to attend the funeral on April 9. There was not enough room for all of them in the church, which could seat only 750 people. Still, 1,000 people managed to somehow squeeze inside.

Another widow made a surprise appearance. It had been just five years since President John F. Kennedy was gunned down during a campaign trip to Dallas, Texas, but Jacqueline Kennedy flew to Atlanta to pay her respects. The sighting of the former First Lady— by then a beloved American icon—sent waves of excitement through the crowd and lent a somber dignity to the proceedings.

But one dignitary did not come to Atlanta. It was President Johnson, who had proclaimed a national day of mourning only two days earlier. Why did LBJ skip his old friend's funeral? Perhaps it was because their friendship and political partnership had ended more than a year earlier in January 1967, when King spoke out against

Jacqueline Kennedy attends the funeral of Martin Luther King, Jr.

the Vietnam War. It might have been because LBJ believed King had betrayed him again in 1968, when he opposed Johnson's nomination and reelection. Perhaps LBJ believed that his attendance—just one week after his stunning announcement that he would not run for another term as president—would cause a media sensation that would detract from the solemnity of the day.

Some critics speculated that LBJ was afraid to come, worrying that someone might attempt to assassinate him. That was not true. Five years earlier LBJ had insisted on walking in President Kennedy's funeral procession, even though the Secret Service argued it was too dangerous. Now LBJ wrestled with this decision. And, at the last minute, he decided not to attend King's funeral. He watched it on

ⓞbsequies

Martin Luther King Jr.

TUESDAY, APRIL 9, 1968

10:30 A. M.

Ebenezer Baptist Church

2:00 P. M.

The Campus of Morehouse College

ATLANTA, GEORGIA

television instead, as did an estimated 120 million people, more than half the population of the United States.

One of those watching was James Earl Ray, holed up in a hotel room in Toronto, Canada. He witnessed the inconsolable sorrow that had caused millions of people to weep, but he did not shed a tear.

The night before his assassination, Martin Luther King, Jr., had called Ralph Abernathy "the best friend I have in the world." Now, in that role, Ralph stepped forward to officiate at his friend's funeral on April 9.

In an eerie touch, King also spoke at his own funeral. Two months earlier, on February 4, 1968, he had given a sermon in which he spoke about his mortality. After so many threats on his life, perhaps it was not odd that King contemplated death and how he wanted to be remembered. His words had been tape-recorded, and Coretta asked that excerpts be played.

Now King's own voice echoed once more through the church where he had in life given so many sermons: "And every now and then I think about my own death, and I think about my own funeral . . . And every now and then I ask myself, 'What I would want said?'"

What, indeed? Did he want to be remembered as the winner of the Nobel Peace Prize or any of his other hundreds of awards? Did he want to be remembered as a bestselling author, or the leader of a cultural movement that changed American history? No, he'd said.

What would this remarkable man want people to think of him?

As King stated in his own words, he wanted to be remembered in a simpler way: "I don't want a long funeral . . . tell them not to talk too long." His disciples ignored that request—the day's memorial events would go on for several hours and last even longer than the funeral ceremonies for President Kennedy.

Martin Luther King said he wanted to be remembered for helping others.

"Yes, if you want to say that I was a drum major, say that I was a drum major for justice. Say that I was a drum major for peace; I was a drum major for righteousness." That was all. "And all the other shallow things will not matter. I won't have any money to leave behind. I won't have the fine and luxurious things of life to leave behind. But I just want to leave a committed life behind."

Widowed mother Coretta Scott King sits on a church pew with her children and brother-in-law A. D. King as they listen to the funeral service.

After the ceremonies at Ebenezer Baptist Church, Martin Luther King, Jr.'s body was taken to Morehouse College, another black college, for a memorial service that could accommodate a larger audience. But he was not driven there in a hearse. Instead, his coffin was drawn through the streets of Atlanta on a farm wagon pulled by two mules, to symbolize the simplicity of the man he was. Thousands of people marched in the procession. "Martin had spent so much of his life marching for justice and freedom, and marching for human dignity," Coretta said in tribute. "This was his last great march."

From left to right: King's daughter Yolanda; King's brother, A. D. King; daughter Bernice; widow, Coretta Scott King; Reverand Ralph Abernathy; and sons, Dexter and Martin Luther III, lead the funeral procession through Atlanta.

Martin Luther King, Jr.'s funeral procession included his coffin on a simple wooden ca pulled by mules.

After the ceremony at Morehouse, his body was finally laid to rest with an entombment service at South-View Cemetery. Here his friend Ralph Abernathy spoke again: "The grave is too narrow for his soul, but we commit his body to the ground. No coffin, no crypt, no vault, no stone can hold his greatness, but we commit his body to the ground." The tombstone was marked with a line from the speech King had delivered at the Lincoln Memorial during the August 1963 March on Washington:

REV. MARTIN LUTHER KING, JR.

1929–1968

"FREE AT LAST, FREE AT LAST,

THANK GOD ALMIGHTY

I'M FREE AT LAST."

But then something strange happened. After the graveside ceremony was over and King's family and associates had departed, bereaved mourners did something bizarre. They wanted to possess a tangible link to their hero, and a few days later, a headline in *JET* magazine revealed what they had done: "Souvenir Seekers Strip Dr. King's Grave." The story reported the details: "A plainclothesman stood guard over the white marble tomb of Dr. Martin Luther King, Jr., urging visitors not to [disturb] the heaps of flowers wilting on the grave. Many of the wreaths were stripped by souvenir seekers shortly after Dr. King was interred . . . but police put a stop to the practice once they took up the watch. South-View Cemetery . . . was sealed off by four officers from midnight to dawn to prevent any tampering with the crypt."

Other souvenirs appeared soon. Pin-back buttons with King's portrait materialized overnight after the assassination and were worn on jacket lapels. Cardboard hand fans bearing King's color portrait and stapled to carrying sticks of cardboard also became popular. For years to come, black-owned businesses across the country printed their logos on the backs of fans and continued to hand them out as keepsakes.

Many people simply cut photos of King from magazines and newspapers and taped them to doors and windows. Memorial signs—some hand-lettered and others professionally printed—appeared in storefronts and the windows of homes. In Chicago, where King had once likened the sting of racism there to anything as vicious as he had ever seen in the South, one company printed attractive memorial portrait banners on black felt. They had done the same thing in 1963 after the Kennedy assassination. Five years later, the company still had boxes of leftover, unsold stock. The reverse side was blank, so they flipped the banners over and printed a tribute to King on the other side.

Many mourners, for the rest of their lives, never took down these photos and banners.

The funeral for Martin Luther King, Jr., was over. But the manhunt for his killer was not. Many questions remained. Who had killed Dr. King? Where was the murderer? And where might he go next?

THE ASSASSIN IDENTIFIED

On Tuesday, April 16, James Earl Ray went to the Kennedy Travel Bureau in Toronto to inquire about buying a ticket to London. When he said he did not have a passport yet, the woman who helped him said she would get it for him. Ray had been under the false impression that he needed a Canadian birth certificate and a witness who had known him for two years to verify his Canadian citizenship.

The woman in the travel bureau informed him that all he had to do was make a sworn statement that he had been born in Canada and sign a notarized document to that effect. Then the travel agency would send in his paperwork and photos and obtain the passport for him. In about two weeks, the passport would be mailed back to the agency. Ray could pick it up there by the beginning of May, along with his ticket to London. It was as easy as that.

But, until he could fly away, Ray had to lie low and avoid the attention of the police. However, in a quirk of fate, he made a trivial mistake that could have ended the manhunt on the spot. A policeman stopped him in the street for jaywalking. He questioned Ray, and then issued him a three-dollar ticket for violating the law.

Ray was lucky that the officer did not ask for identification. He was still carrying ID for Eric S. Galt, one of the names the FBI had released that very day as a suspect in the assassination of Dr. King.

The FBI investigation had made great progress. Clues in California led them to the National Dance Studio in Long Beach and the bartending school in Los Angeles. At the school, agents obtained a copy of Ray's graduation photo, the one in which he had closed his eyes just before the picture was taken. Locating the photo was a small victory, although Ray's clever trick did make it harder to recognize him. To make identification of the suspect easier, an artist painted eyes into the picture. Although the FBI lab had still not matched the fingerprints it had collected to any known records in its database, Hoover and DeLoach decided to go public, announcing a warrant for the arrest of Eric Starvo Galt.

So, on April 17, thirteen days after the assassination, the FBI published its first wanted poster for the assassin of Martin Luther King. The posters were mailed to and displayed nationwide in post offices, which were community meeting points that people often visited in their daily lives. This placement ensured that millions would see them.

The poster included two versions of the photo of Ray from his bartending school graduation, one with his eyes closed as well as one in which the FBI had painted his eyes open. Flyer 442 stated that Eric Starvo Galt was wanted by the FBI. It read:

"CAUTION: GALT IS SOUGHT IN CONNECTION WITH A MURDER WHEREIN THE VICTIM WAS SHOT. CONSIDER ARMED AND EXTREMELY DANGEROUS."

WANTED

CIVIL RIGHTS - CONSPIRACY
ERIC STARVO GALT

FBI No. 405,942 G

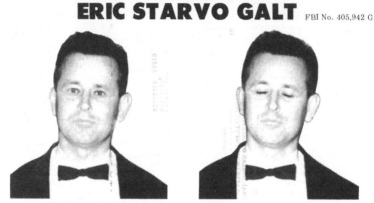

Photograph taken 1968
(eyes drawn by artist)

Photograph taken 1968

Aliases: Harvey Lowmyer, John Willard

DESCRIPTION

Age:	36, born July 20, 1931 (not supported by birth records)		
Height:	5'8" to 5'11"	**Eyes:**	Blue or hazel
Weight:	160 to 175 pounds	**Complexion:**	Medium
Build:	Medium	**Race:**	White
Hair:	Brown, possibly cut short		
Occupation:	Has claimed employment as seaman		
Remarks:	Noticeably protruding left ear; reportedly is a lone wolf; allegedly attended dance instruction school; has reportedly completed course in bartending.		

CAUTION

GALT IS SOUGHT IN CONNECTION WITH A MURDER WHEREIN THE VICTIM WAS SHOT. CONSIDER ARMED AND EXTREMELY DANGEROUS.

A Federal warrant was issued on April 17, 1968, at Birmingham, Alabama, charging Galt with conspiring to interfere with a Constitutional Right of a citizen (Title 18, U. S. Code, Section 241).

IF YOU HAVE ANY INFORMATION CONCERNING THIS PERSON, PLEASE NOTIFY ME OR CONTACT YOUR LOCAL FBI OFFICE. TELEPHONE NUMBERS AND ADDRESSES OF ALL FBI OFFICES LISTED ON BACK.

DIRECTOR
FEDERAL BUREAU OF INVESTIGATION
UNITED STATES DEPARTMENT OF JUSTICE
WASHINGTON, D. C. 20535
TELEPHONE, NATIONAL 8-7117

Wanted Flyer 442
April 17, 1968

The first FBI wanted poster for King's assassin, James Earl Ray. The FBI had tracked down a photo of the suspected killer, who was known to the FBI under a false name, Eric

Strangely, the poster never stated that Galt was wanted specifically for the assassination of Dr. King. That was because murder was not a federal crime and therefore was not within the jurisdiction of the FBI. However, by linking Galt to a violation of civil rights, the FBI could properly investigate.

Then the FBI struck gold. Its fingerprint lab finally identified the prints collected in Memphis—they belonged to James Earl Ray, prison escapee.

This had not been an easy process. In an age before digital images and computer searches, agents had to visually compare thousands of fingerprints by hand. On April 19, the FBI released a second wanted poster, the first to name James Earl Ray as the assassin:

"Wanted flyer 442-A. For Civil Rights - Conspiracy - Interstate Flight - Robbery. Remarks: 'Noticeably protruding left ear; reportedly is a lone wolf; allegedly attended dance instruction school; has reportedly completed a course in bartending.'" The poster printed three photos, two of them mug shots taken of Ray in 1960, and the other, the bartending school photograph with the eyes painted in.

The next day, on April 20, the FBI published a third wanted poster that also named Ray, included three photos, and, for the first time, a full set of Ray's fingerprints.

The positive identification of James Earl Ray as King's killer just fifteen days after the crime was one of the FBI's finest triumphs. Now they knew the subject of their manhunt.

But where was he?

Four American presidents have been assassinated: Abraham Lincoln, James Garfield, William McKinley, and John F. Kennedy.

WANTED BY THE FBI

CIVIL RIGHTS - CONSPIRACY
INTERSTATE FLIGHT - ROBBERY
JAMES EARL RAY

FBI No. 405,942 G

Photographs taken 1960

Photograph taken 1968
(eyes drawn by artist)

Aliases: Eric Starvo Galt, W. C. Herron, Harvey Lowmyer, James McBride, James O'Conner, James Walton, James Walyon, John Willard, "Jim,"

DESCRIPTION

Age:	40, born March 10, 1928, at Quincy or Alton, Illinois (not supported by birth records)		
Height:	5' 10"	**Eyes:**	Blue
Weight:	163 to 174 pounds	**Complexion:**	Medium
Build:	Medium	**Race:**	White
Hair:	Brown, possibly cut short	**Nationality:**	American

Occupations: Baker, color matcher, laborer

Scars and Marks: Small scar on center of forehead and small scar on palm of right hand

Remarks: Noticeably protruding left ear; reportedly is a lone wolf; allegedly attended dance instruction school; has reportedly completed course in bartending.

Fingerprint Classification: 16 M 9 U OOO 12
M 4 W I OI

CRIMINAL RECORD

Ray has been convicted of burglary, robbery, forging U. S. Postal Money Orders, armed robbery, and operating motor vehicle without owner's consent.

CAUTION

RAY IS SOUGHT IN CONNECTION WITH A MURDER WHEREIN THE VICTIM WAS SHOT. CONSIDER ARMED AND EXTREMELY DANGEROUS.

A Federal warrant was issued on April 17, 1968, at Birmingham, Alabama, charging Ray as Eric Starvo Galt with conspiring to interfere with a Constitutional Right of a citizen (Title 18, U. S. Code, Section 241). A Federal warrant was also issued on July 20, 1967, at Jefferson City, Missouri, charging Ray with Interstate Flight to Avoid Confinement for the crime of Robbery (Title 18, U. S. Code, Section 1073).

IF YOU HAVE ANY INFORMATION CONCERNING THIS PERSON, PLEASE NOTIFY ME OR CONTACT YOUR LOCAL FBI OFFICE. TELEPHONE NUMBERS AND ADDRESSES OF ALL FBI OFFICES LISTED ON BACK.

J. Edgar Hoover

DIRECTOR
FEDERAL BUREAU OF INVESTIGATION
UNITED STATES DEPARTMENT OF JUSTICE
WASHINGTON, D. C. 20535
TELEPHONE, NATIONAL 8-7117

Wanted Flyer 442-A
April 19, 1968

The second FBI wanted poster for King's killer. By now, the FBI had correctly identified Ray and had obtained a mug shot and a list of his aliases.

The third version of the FBI wanted poster included mug shots and photos of Ray's fingerprints.

Garfield's and McKinley's killers had been captured immediately at the scenes of their crimes. And Lee Harvey Oswald had been captured within two hours of killing Kennedy. Even Lincoln's assassin, John Wilkes Booth, had been hunted down and killed after a twelve-day manhunt. King's murder was as high profile as the assassination of any American president. So why hadn't Ray been captured? People expected quick action and decisive results.

The next night, April 21, James Earl Ray was sitting in a bar in Toronto, Canada, watching the popular American TV show *The F.B.I.,* starring Efrem Zimbalist, Jr., as Inspector Lewis Erskine. After each weekly episode, Zimbalist would appear on-screen to discuss one of the FBI's current cases. That night, he requested the public's help in apprehending the fugitive James Earl Ray for the assassination of Dr. Martin Luther King, Jr.

Ray had always been a fan of the TV show. He had gone to four bars, looking for one that was tuned to the program, in the hopes that he would see his own face on the screen. He wanted to know if he had made it onto the Ten Most Wanted list.

He had.

The FBI knew it was him. Ray realized that he had to get out of Canada. Having hidden in Toronto for almost a full month, Ray decided to catch a flight to London on May 6.

But London was not his first choice. He had wanted to fly to Africa, to a country that did not have an extradition treaty with the United States. However, the price of a round-trip ticket was about $820. At the time, you could not fly into such countries without a return ticket, and Ray didn't have enough money. Ray had only about $800.

There was only one way that Ray could get a lot of money fast—he could commit a robbery. But he was afraid of getting caught. "That's where I made my mistake," Ray said. "I should have pulled a holdup. But I didn't. And I let myself get on that plane to London without enough money to get where I intended to go."

So Ray arrived in Great Britain early on May 7, but he didn't even leave Heathrow Airport.

"Upon my arrival in England I . . . used my return ticket to Canada to go to Portugal that night," Ray said. "I didn't want to spend any more time in London than I had to."

Ray arrived in Lisbon, Portugal, early on May 8. His plan was to find a ship sailing from Portugal to Angola, a former Portuguese colony, where he planned to become a mercenary—a soldier for hire—for whatever cause would pay him.

But there was a problem. It would take seven days to get a visa to travel to Angola. By that time, the ship would be gone. Ray was so short of money that he decided to head back to London, where he might find other options.

On May 17, Ray flew from Lisbon back to London. What to do now?

He was not there as a tourist; he was not there to see the sights of the historic city. Instead, he holed up and hunkered down. He rented a small, inexpensive room on the outskirts of the city center, but he rarely went out during the day, afraid to leave because he worried that he might be identified. At night, he went out to buy food and newspapers, so he could read what the press was saying about the assassination. But he was running low on money, paying each day for room and food without any income.

On May 27, desperate and with his landlady demanding rent money that he didn't have, Ray tried to rob a jewelry store owned by a married couple. But they turned the tables on Ray and attacked him—the wife jumped on his back and the husband pummeled him in the face! They set off the store alarm, and Ray ran away.

In the meantime, the FBI had learned that Ray had visited Canada after his 1967 escape from prison. The Bureau asked Canadian officials to examine all passport applications from the past year to see if Ray had applied for one. It was a daunting task; a dozen officers had to examine more than 200,000 applications by hand.

On June 1, one passport application caught a constable's eye. The applicant's photograph resembled images of James Earl Ray provided by the FBI.

Was it really him? Had they found King's killer?

NAME · NOM

MR. RAMON GEORGE SNEYD

BIRTHDATE · DATE DE NAISSANCE

8 OCTOBER 1932

BIRTHPLACE · LIEU DE NAISSANCE

TORONTO, ONTARIO

HEIGHT · TAILLE

5 FEET
PIEDS 10 INCHES
POUCES

HAIR · CHEVEUX

BLACK

EYES · YEUX

BLUE

PASSPORT ISSUED AT · CE PASSEPORT DÉLIVRÉ À

LISBON, PORTUGAL

CHILDREN · ENFANTS

BIRTHDATE · NÉ LE

ON · LE

MAY 16, 1968

PASSPORT EXPIRES · CE PASSEPORT EXPIRE

24 APRIL 1973

4-1-A

See information on inside back cover.   Voir l'Avis en troisième page de couverture.

RENEWALS
PROROGATIONS

3

PHOTOGRAPH OF BEARER
PHOTOGRAPHIE DU TITULAIRE

This passport is hereby renewed valid until
Ce passeport est prorogé jusqu'au

Ramon George Sneyl

Ramon George Sneyd

Signature of bearer - Signature du titulaire

The first passport contained an error. It misspelled the last name as "Sneya" instead of "Sney
Ray obtained a corrected version of the passport from the Canadian consulate in Portugal.

ANOTHER ASSASSINATION AND AN ARREST

The search for King's killer was up until then the largest and most expensive manhunt in FBI history. Three thousand agents—almost half the strength of the FBI—had been deployed on the case. They had learned much. They had confirmed that James Earl Ray—despite his many aliases—was, in fact, Martin Luther King's killer. They had investigated his prior arrests and imprisonments, and had worked to discover his movements since he had escaped from prison in April 1967. They had reconstructed Ray's life by interviewing his family, friends, and people who had once known or met him. Wherever the FBI had found potential clues, they had pursued them diligently. In fact, wherever James Earl Ray had been, the FBI had followed.

But by June, the American people had grown impatient with the FBI's lack of progress. Weeks had passed without any fresh leads. Martin Luther King, Jr., had been murdered almost two months ago. Why was James Earl Ray still on the run? Where was he? Why hadn't the FBI tracked him down yet?

President Johnson and J. Edgar Hoover were also frustrated. The delay fueled rumors of a conspiracy. No other American assassin had been a fugitive—despite the international manhunt under way—for so long. In the rogues' gallery of the country's most notorious killers, James Earl Ray had managed to stay on the run and elude capture longer, and travel farther, than any assassin in American history.

But by June 4, Ray was down to his last ten pounds sterling. Desperate times called for desperate measures. Wearing dark sunglasses as a disguise, he walked into a bank and, pointing a pistol at the teller, shoved forward a handwritten note demanding money. The teller handed over some cash, but then kicked over a metal box that made a loud bang. The sound startled everyone in the bank, including Ray. He fled immediately, chased by two of the bank tellers but managed to escape. However, he left behind an important clue: the note written in his own hand.

That wasn't the only evidence he left; the note bore an identifiable thumbprint.

For all his trouble, the robbery only netted about the equivalent of $240—not nearly enough to finance a trip to Africa. And there was a bigger problem that Ray couldn't yet know: When Canadian officials confirmed that Ray indeed had applied for a passport, they immediately went to the travel agency that had gotten it for him. When questioned, the agency revealed that Ray had bought a ticket to London, so Britain's famed Scotland Yard was put on the case.

Detectives discovered that Ray had flown from London to Portugal but had then come back to London. Without finding any trace of Ray having flown elsewhere, they concluded that Dr. King's assassin was still on the loose in Britain.

Meanwhile, in America, the two-month anniversary of King's death also fell on June 4. Late that evening, after midnight on the West Coast, stunning news came out of California. Most Americans were already asleep when it was announced. In Washington, DC, and along the East Coast, it was already past 3:00 a.m., Eastern Standard Time. The majority of Americans did not hear the news until the morning of June 5, when they turned on their televisions, listened to their radios, or opened their newspapers, the three main ways people got the news in 1968.

But it was not the good news that James Earl Ray had been found and captured. It was bad news.

There had been another assassination.

Senator Robert Kennedy had been shot.

Kennedy was at the Ambassador Hotel in Los Angeles, at a political rally to celebrate his victory in the California Democratic presidential primary. The senator left the ballroom by a back exit and was led through the hotel's pantry and kitchen. A man lurking there stepped forward and began firing wildly with a .22-caliber revolver, wounding several people, including Kennedy. The senator had been shot three times. Two of the wounds did not seem to be life-threatening.

But the third wound was serious. Like his brother, President John F. Kennedy, Robert Kennedy had been shot in the brain. The parallels were eerie. Like Martin Luther King, Robert Kennedy had been shot at a hotel. This, another tragedy, following the King

Presidential candidate Senator Robert F. Kennedy, felled by an assassin's bullets, lie
bleeding on the floor of the kitchen of the Ambassador Hotel in Los Angeles, Californi
just after midnight on June 5, 1968. A hotel busboy comforts Kennedy

assassination by only eight weeks, was a staggering blow almost too great for the nation to bear.

Robert Kennedy died the next day, after midnight on June 6, about twenty-six hours after he was shot. Soon, Jackie Kennedy would put on another black suit, just like the one she had worn after her husband, President Kennedy, was slain in 1963. Soon she would attend another funeral. Americans asked themselves what kind of country theirs was becoming. And what tragedy might happen next?

In London, in a time zone several hours ahead of the United States, James Earl Ray might have learned the news before most of the American people had gotten out of bed. This was not good news for Ray. Public outrage over the Kennedy assassination was sure to intensify the manhunt for him. It was time, Ray decided, to get out of England, and he knew exactly where he wanted to go.

On June 7, Ray bought a one-way plane ticket from London to Brussels, Belgium, departing the next day. He wanted to make connections with the shadowy world of paramilitary mercenaries. From Brussels, he wanted to fly to Africa and work as a soldier for hire in a white-ruled English-speaking country like Rhodesia that would never deport him to the United States.

If James Earl Ray had escaped to Africa, he might have vanished and never been captured.

But Ray did not know a critical fact. Two days earlier, Scotland Yard had placed the name of Ramon George Sneyd—Ray's alias— on a travel restriction list. Now immigration officials in every airport and seaport knew his name.

And they were looking for him.

Back in the United States, mourning continued. Full-color, machine-woven tapestries portraying John Kennedy, Martin Luther King, and Robert Kennedy appeared in homes across America. The wall hanging was like an iconic religious triptych of America's three recently martyred secular saints. Publishers issued magazine tributes to the three widows, Jacqueline Kennedy, Coretta Scott King, and Ethel Kennedy, depicting them on the front covers, united in sorrow. And fan makers created a new design featuring King and the two Kennedys, with the printed legend: FREEDOM FIGHTERS.

Because Robert Kennedy had been a United States senator from New York State, his body was flown from Los Angeles to New York City for funeral ceremonies there. Then, on June 8, his coffin was placed aboard a special train that would carry him to the nation's capital, for burial at Arlington National Cemetery beside his brother.

On June 8, James Earl Ray caught a taxi to Heathrow Airport to make his 11:15 a.m. flight. After checking his bag at the ticket counter, he proceeded to the customs and immigration checkpoint. An official requested his passport. Ray removed it from his wallet. Upon inspection, everything seemed to be in order. The officer was about to wave him through when he spotted something strange: a *second* passport protruding from Ray's wallet.

"May I see the other one?" he asked. Ray explained that it was his first Canadian passport, which he had replaced because it had spelled his (assumed) name incorrectly. Ray's story seemed to satisfy the officer. In just a few minutes, Ray would get on the plane and escape England. But at that moment, a Scotland Yard detective, Philip Birch, appeared and overheard the conversation. Ray looked familiar. But the officer did not know why. In fact, the *Police Gazette*, a newsletter for law officers, had published a photo of Ray.

"I say, old fellow," Birch asked, "would you mind stepping over here for a moment? I'd like to have a word with you." Ray protested that his plane was leaving soon, but Birch promised it would not take long. He and two officers escorted Ray to a police office at the airport. Then Birch caught Ray by surprise and asked, "Would you mind if I searched you?"

Ray was in danger now. A search would reveal that he carried a pistol in his pants pocket. This was Ray's last chance to put up a fight before the police discovered the weapon. He would have to pull out the pistol and try to shoot his way out of the airport. But he did not resist and submitted to the search.

"Why are you carrying this gun?" Birch demanded. "Well," Ray answered, "I am going to Africa, I thought I might need it. You know how things are there." Two other investigators arrived and asked if he had a permit to possess the pistol. Ray admitted he did not, and was duly arrested for unlawful possession of a firearm. He was taken back to London, where he was fingerprinted and locked in a cell at Scotland Yard. He would not make his flight to Brussels after all.

Later that afternoon, after further investigation, Detective Chief Superintendent Thomas Butler confronted Ray. "We have very good reason to believe that you are not a Canadian citizen, but an American." Ray admitted the truth: "Oh, well, yes I am." Butler continued: "I now believe your name is not Sneyd, but James Earl Ray, also known as Eric Starvo Galt . . ." He added that Ray was wanted in the United States for murder. At that moment, Ray broke down completely. "Oh, God," he said weakly, "I feel so trapped."

Butler cautioned Ray that anything he said could be used against him, to which Ray replied, "Yes, I shouldn't say anything more now. I can't think right."

On June 8, in America, television coverage of the Kennedy funeral events was interrupted by a special bulletin from faraway London. The news was electrifying.

James Earl Ray had been captured. The manhunt for Dr. Martin Luther King's assassin was over!

Extradition proceedings—a court action to return a suspect to the jurisdiction where he allegedly committed a crime—lasted several weeks and delayed Ray's return to the United States. It wasn't until July 18 that Ray was handed over to FBI agents in London and

Despite King's death, the Poor People's Campaign marched on Washington, DC, that summer. Participants, who called their encampment Resurrection City, read the news of Ray's capture.

flown back to America aboard a military aircraft. Ray was brought back to Memphis, the scene of his crime, on July 19. It had been an odyssey of a little more than one hundred and six days from King's assassination to Ray's extradition from England. It had been a fifteen-month journey from the date of Ray's escape from prison in April 1967 to his capture and return to Memphis in July 1968.

So the manhunt was over. But the mystery was not. James Earl Ray refused to confess. He wanted to go to trial, and he sought representation by F. Lee Bailey, the most famous defense attorney at that time, who specialized in high-profile criminal and murder cases. Ray expected—with the help of first-rate lawyering—to be acquitted, believing that no white jury in the South would ever convict him. Ray deluded himself into believing that many Americans

James Earl Ray, manacled and wearing a bulletproof apron, is brought into Shelby Count Jail, Memphis, Tennessee, July 19, 1968. He had eluded capture for around two months

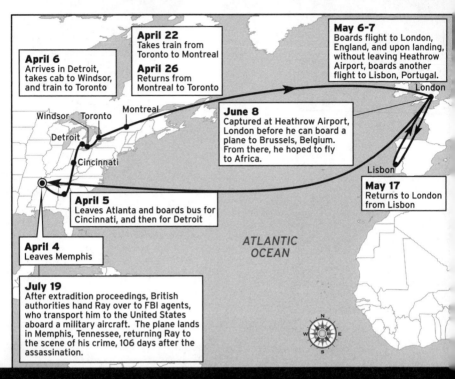

April 6
Arrives in Detroit, takes cab to Windsor, and train to Toronto

April 22
Takes train from Toronto to Montreal

April 26
Returns from Montreal to Toronto

May 6-7
Boards flight to London, England, and upon landing, without leaving Heathrow Airport, boards another flight to Lisbon, Portugal.

June 8
Captured at Heathrow Airport, London before he can board a plane to Brussels, Belgium. From there, he hoped to fly to Africa.

May 17
Returns to London from Lisbon

April 5
Leaves Atlanta and boards bus for Cincinnati, and then for Detroit

April 4
Leaves Memphis

July 19
After extradition proceedings, British authorities hand Ray over to FBI agents, who transport him to the United States aboard a military aircraft. The plane lands in Memphis, Tennessee, returning Ray to the scene of his crime, 106 days after the assassination.

Windsor Toronto Montreal
Detroit
Cincinnati
London
Lisbon

ATLANTIC OCEAN

Map of Ray's movements from escape to capture.

would treat him as a hero, and that once he had been acquitted he could make money from his infamy. Americans wanted a trial, too, not because they wished to see Ray go free but because it would provide a relief when all the facts of the crime were revealed. But Bailey wanted nothing to do with Ray, and the rejection surprised him.

Ray involved himself with a series of publicity-seeking lawyers who conducted lackluster investigations, did inadequate pretrial preparation, and pursued crazy and unethical schemes to make money from book deals and magazine articles about Ray. They seemed more interested in what Ray could do for them than what they could do for him.

Amid this chaos and circus-like atmosphere, Ray eventually pled guilty because he wanted to avoid the death penalty. There would be no trial. He was sentenced to ninety-nine years in prison. The American people and the national news media were stunned. It was not, they argued, in the public interest for this case to end without a trial. How else could all the facts of the King assassination ever be made known, except by a comprehensive investigation and a public prosecution in open court?

In this vacuum, conspiracy theories abounded. This was similar to what had happened five years earlier, after the assassination of President Kennedy. These theories blamed King's murder on everyone from J. Edgar Hoover and the FBI, to other government entities, to the Ku Klux Klan and white racists. One of King's associates claimed that there was no way a "ten-cent white man" could pull off the murder of a "million-dollar black man" on his own. Someone, he argued, had to have helped or guided Ray.

The conspiracy question has several elements. Some theorists argue that another assassin, not James Earl Ray, fired the shot that killed Martin Luther King. But no evidence of this has ever been found, while compelling evidence exists to prove that it was Ray. Other conspiracy advocates, conceding that Ray was the gunman, claim that he was a hired assassin paid by conspirators who had offered a reward to anyone who killed King. But no evidence of this has ever been found. Later, Ray had second thoughts and tried to retract his plea, claiming that he was only a pawn or puppet of the real killers. Ray claimed that a mysterious man who went by the name Raoul organized the murder, but such a man could never be located or even identified, and strong evidence suggests that he was just a lie that Ray invented in an attempt to exonerate himself.

If Ray was a lone wolf who really planned the assassination by himself, did he receive help from conspirators after the fact, from persons unknown who helped him while he was on the run? Ray's long and far-flung escape raised questions. How did he do it? How did he get so far? How did Martin Luther King's assassin stay on the run for two months? How did he escape the United States? Where did he get money to travel and obtain a fraudulent passport? How did he get all the way to England?

These questions all have answers.

Based on extensive physical evidence and eyewitness testimony, there is no doubt that James Earl Ray was the assassin. Only one man could have fired the shot from the bathroom of the rooming house on Main Street. It was Ray, and he is the man who killed Dr. Martin Luther King, Jr.

It was James Earl Ray who bought the rifle. It was Ray who checked into the New Rebel Motel on the night of April 3, 1968. It was Ray who checked into the rooming house opposite the Lorraine Motel on April 4. It was Ray who left behind evidence and fingerprints, all pointing to him. It was Ray's white Mustang seen fleeing the scene of the crime and found later containing additional evidence. It was Ray who fled to Canada and forged a passport. And it was Ray who fled to Europe and was captured in London, precisely because he did not have the money to escape to Africa.

There is no evidence that it was anyone else but James Earl Ray who assassinated Martin Luther King, Jr.

But *why* did Ray do it? The answer to that question remains a frustrating mystery.

It seems obvious that James Earl Ray did not escape from prison in April 1967 in order to kill Martin Luther King, Jr. For almost a year after Ray's breakout, he did nothing to show that he had the slightest interest in murdering anyone, including King. He did not behave like a would-be assassin—he did not stalk King immediately, buy a rifle earlier, or move to the South right away. None of Ray's activities show evidence that he was obsessed with Martin Luther King or planned to harm him.

Was it for fame? For all of his life, Ray had been the kind of man who preferred to live in the shadows. He craved anonymity, not attention. It was out of character for him to seek notoriety. On the other hand, some evidence suggests that, in the end he wanted to leave his mark by doing something "big" in his hitherto insignificant life.

Was it for ideological reasons? Ray was a racist and white supremacist, like millions of other Americans at that time, but were those reasons enough for him to uproot his life in California and travel across the country to kill a man? Ray was a loner and had never been a joiner. He had never been a member of the Ku Klux Klan or a racial agitator. He had never participated in public protests against blacks, never shown up to harass civil rights demonstrators, and had never burned a cross or thrown a rock.

It might have been about money.

One of Ray's brothers once said that James never did anything if it wasn't for money. Ray's life of low-end crime supports that view. For several years prior to the assassination, rumors had circulated through the South that wealthy racists in various states had placed cash bounties on Martin Luther King, Jr., and were willing to pay big money—even fifty or one hundred thousand dollars—to the man who killed him. It is hard to believe that Ray assassinated King for a cause. But for money? That seems possible. Money *was* James Earl Ray's cause. Was Ray after one of those rumored rewards? Did he actually seek out and make contact with someone who had offered one?

It is impossible to know, and Ray never said.

A YEAR LIKE NO OTHER

In August 1968, the pop singer Dion released a song that seemed to encapsulate the trauma that the American people had suffered. Written by Dick Holler and sung by Dion, the single, titled "Abraham, Martin and John," referenced the murdered leaders Abraham Lincoln, John Kennedy, Martin Luther King, and Robert Kennedy.

The first verse invoked Lincoln's assassination on April 14, 1865; the second verse the assassination of John Kennedy on November 22, 1963; and the third verse the April 4 assassination of Martin Luther King, just four months earlier. As the lyrics went:

> Anybody here seen my old friend Martin?
> Can you tell me where he's gone?
> He freed lotta people but it seems the good they die young.
> I just looked around and he's gone.

The final verse honored Robert Kennedy, who had been shot only weeks earlier. The song became an instant hit and reached number four on the U.S. pop singles chart. In late summer and early fall

ABRAHAM, MARTIN and JOHN

Words and Music by DICK HOLLER

ROZNIQUE MUSIC, INC. / 8th Floor — 17 West 60th St., New York, N.Y. 10023   85¢

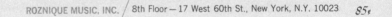

Sheet music for the song "Abraham, Martin and John." John F. Kennedy, Martin Luther King, Jr., and Robert Kennedy have replaced George Washington, Thomas Jefferson, and Theodore Roosevelt as they join Abraham Lincoln on Mount Rushmore.

1968, it seemed impossible to turn on the radio without hearing "Abraham, Martin and John." The lyrics resonated with an America in mourning, but also with a country looking to move forward from such tragedies. As one verse predicted:

Didn't you love the things that they stood for?
Didn't they try to find some good for you and me?
And we'll be free.
Some day soon, it's gonna be one day.

It was one of those songs that defined a moment in time and captured the mood of a nation. Even today, when someone who remembers the King assassination hears that song, the emotions come flooding back. Later, it was awarded a Recording Industry Association of America gold record for selling more than one million copies.

The nation mourned and the seasons passed. Summer turned to fall, and American casualties in the Vietnam War continued to rise. And after Richard Nixon won the November presidential election, 1968 drew to a close. It had been an incredible year of unrest, violence, and uncertainty. There was the surprise Tet Offensive in Vietnam, public protests, chaos in the streets, assassinations, riots, and cities in flames. There had been death, inconsolable sadness, and tears. It had been one of the most tumultuous years in American history.

Americans looked to the heavens to transcend the chaos of what was happening on Earth. On December 21, 1968, NASA launched Apollo 8, the first manned mission to orbit the moon.

The planet Earth as seen from Apollo 8, December 1968, showing the earthrise—"a jewel hanging in the blackness of space."

As they circled sixty miles above the lunar surface, the astronauts aboard Apollo 8 witnessed what no humans had ever seen, the entire planet Earth from space, and then they took one of the most iconic photographs in the history of space exploration: "Earthrise," a striking color image of mankind's home planet rising above the horizon of the moon. One of the Apollo astronauts marveled that Earth looked like "a jewel hanging in the blackness of space." On Christmas Eve, as Apollo 8 orbited the moon, the crew—Frank Borman, Jim Lovell, and Bill Anders—took turns reading aloud the first ten verses from the Old Testament book of Genesis, and a radio transmitted their voices 235,000 miles back to Earth.

And so the troubled year of 1968 ended on a melancholy note of consolation and hope: "In the beginning God created the heaven and the earth. And the earth was without form, and void; and darkness was upon the face of the deep. And the spirit of God moved upon the face of the waters. And God said, Let there be light: and there was light. And God saw the light, that it was good: and God divided the light from the darkness."

After the crew finished reading the remaining verses, Jim Lovell said farewell: "And from the crew of Apollo 8, we close with good night, good luck, a Merry Christmas, and God bless all of you—all of you on the good Earth."

Americans turned their eyes skyward, and the marvels of what they saw there helped overcome some of the real pain and suffering on Earth by bringing together so many people in new shared wonder.

But how could the country and its people recover from the death of Dr. Martin Luther King, Jr.?

It is hard to believe that the assassination of Dr. Martin Luther King, Jr., happened half a century ago. In April 2018, America commemorates the fiftieth anniversary of his death. King had titled one of his books *Where Do We Go from Here?* Today, it seems fitting to ask, "Where have we come since then?"

If Martin Luther King had survived that day in Memphis, it is possible that, had he been given the gift of years, he might still be alive today. In April 2018, on the fiftieth anniversary of his assassination, Martin Luther King would have been eighty-nine years old.

If he were alive today, what would his message be?

He had won many of his most important battles. Yes, the old legal impediments of a nation that perpetuated racial segregation in education, housing, public transportation, restaurants, employment, and other areas of American life all came tumbling down. But that was not enough. There is more to civil rights than just overturning racist laws and passing new laws to protect those rights. One subject dear to King—economic justice—remains a major and hotly debated issue in our time. King would speak to us about it with passion and eloquence because he believed that true equality was not possible without economic opportunity and prosperity.

If he were alive today, Martin Luther King, Jr., would also speak about disparities in employment and criminal justice. New civil rights issues have arisen in our own time, including the Black Lives Matter movement, voter ID and voting rights concerns, and racially motivated shootings. King would be disappointed that, in many places and cultures around the world, the human and civil rights of many people—especially young girls and women—are violated every day. But he would have been amazed and delighted that in 2008, an African American had been elected president of the United States. That is part of King's legacy, too.

In Washington, DC, you can visit memorials to three murdered American heroes. Abraham Lincoln sits in his marble columned memorial on the National Mall. John F. Kennedy's eternal flame burns at his grave at Arlington Cemetery. And a new, monumental sculpture of Martin Luther King, Jr., larger than life, has risen to join them.

All were great men, all were inspirations in their own times, and remain so today. If you visit them at night when their memorials contrast dramatically against the dark sky, it is hard to forget Dr. King's last wish, which Lincoln and Kennedy would have certainly shared: "Like anybody, I would like to live."

And so their legacies live on: Lincoln, savior of a nation founded on a flawed experiment in liberty for some but not all, and who ended slavery but did not live long enough to guarantee the civil rights of the slaves he freed; Kennedy, who thought that racial

The colossal Martin Luther King, Jr., memorial in Washington, DC, stands near the
Lincoln Memorial and across the Potomac River from John F. Kennedy's grave.

oppression at home undermined America's moral force on the world stage; and King, the prophet who sought to redeem America from the flawed, unjust, and violent century that followed the Civil War.

Perhaps you are also wondering what happened to some of the other people you have read about in this book.

In 1969, it was revealed that Robert F. Kennedy had authorized J. Edgar Hoover's FBI wiretap surveillance of Dr. King. *JET* magazine, a leading African American publication, expressed the shock and disappointment felt throughout the black community. Kennedy was no longer alive to explain himself, and his reputation suffered.

On May 2, 1972, King's old nemesis, J. Edgar Hoover, died peacefully in his sleep. He was seventy-seven years old, and he had been the director since 1935, for the entire existence of the FBI. He never repented his harassment of Martin Luther King, but he was proud of the outstanding work that his FBI had done in tracking down King's assassin. At the agency he once ruled with an iron fist, Hoover had fallen from grace. Recently, the FBI office in New York City removed a wax figure of Hoover from public display and placed it in permanent storage.

On January 22, 1973, four years after he left the White House, President Lyndon B. Johnson died of a heart attack. He was sixty-four. He and King had not reconciled before King's death. The wounds were too deep. But in LBJ's last public remarks, given at a civil rights symposium at his presidential library shortly before he died, he must have had his old friend Martin in mind when he spoke the inspiring words from that great civil rights anthem: "We shall overcome."

In 1974, six years after the assassination, Martin Luther King's family suffered another tragedy. On the morning of Sunday, June 30, King's sixty-nine-year-old mother, Alberta, was playing the organ at Atlanta's Ebenezer Baptist Church. A crazed twenty-three-year-old black man stormed in and opened fire with a pistol, hitting three people. He shot Alberta King in the head. Later, the attacker confessed that he had wanted to kill Martin Luther King's father, but Mrs. King was closer and was an easier target, so he decided to shoot and kill her. The gunman also shot two more church members, killing one.

Reverand Martin Luther King, Sr., had lost both his son and his wife to assassins; it was more than any person should have to bear.

Meanwhile, James Earl Ray was restless behind bars. He did not want to spend the rest of his life in prison. He tried several times to escape but failed each time. In 1977, however, he succeeded, escaping from Tennessee's Brushy Mountain State Penitentiary. But his freedom was short-lived. After his first prison escape in 1967, he had stayed on the run for more than a year. The FBI issued another reward poster; this time he was recaptured in just three days.

James Earl Ray was recaptured after having been on the run for

WANTED

BY THE FBI

CONSPIRACY; INTERSTATE FLIGHT - ESCAPE
JAMES EARL RAY

Photographs taken 1975

FBI No. 405,942 G

Aliases: Paul Bridgeman, Eric Starvo Galt, W. C. Herron, Harvey Lowmyer, James McBride, James O'Conner, Raymond George Sneyd, James Walton, James Walyon, John Willard, "Jim," and others.

DESCRIPTION

Age: 49, born March 10, 1928, Quincy or Alton, Illinois (not supported by birth records)
Height: 5'10"
Weight: 170 pounds
Build: Medium
Hair: Black, graying
Eyes: Blue
Complexion: Medium
Race: White
Nationality: American
Occupations: Baker, color matcher, laborer
Scars and Marks: Small scar on center of forehead and small scar on palm of right hand.
Remarks: Noticeably protruding left ear; reportedly a lone wolf; allegedly attended dance instruction school; reportedly completed course in bartending.
Social Security Number Used: 334-22-6876

Fingerprint Classification: 16 M 9 U OOO 12 Ref: 9
M 4 W I O I 12
NCIC: 16 13 11 PO 12 12 DI 13 PI 17

CRIMINAL RECORD

Ray has been convicted of murder, burglary, robbery, forging U. S. Postal money orders, armed robbery, operating motor vehicle without owner's consent.

CAUTION

RAY, AT TIME OF ESCAPE, WAS SERVING A NINETY-NINE-YEAR SENTENCE FOLLOWING HIS CONVICTION FOR 1ST DEGREE MURDER WHEREIN A FIREARM WAS USED. CONSIDER ARMED AND EXTREMELY DANGEROUS.

A Federal warrant was issued on June 11, 1977, at Knoxville, Tennessee, charging Ray with conspiracy to violate the Unlawful Flight Statute (Title 18, U. S. Code, Section 371, and Title 18, U. S. Code, Section 1073.)

IF YOU HAVE ANY INFORMATION CONCERNING THIS PERSON, PLEASE NOTIFY ME OR CONTACT YOUR LOCAL FBI OFFICE. TELEPHONE NUMBERS AND ADDRESSES OF ALL FBI OFFICES LISTED ON BACK.

C. M. Kelley

DIRECTOR
FEDERAL BUREAU OF INVESTIGATION
UNITED STATES DEPARTMENT OF JUSTICE
WASHINGTON, D. C. 20535
TELEPHONE: 202 324-3000

Entered NCIC
Wanted Flyer 500
June 11, 1977

FBI wanted poster issued after Ray's 1977 escape from Tennessee's Brushy Mountain State Prison.

For the rest of his life, Ray sowed confusion and spread disinformation about the assassination. In 1978, he even testified before Congress, appearing before a joint committee. Ignoring the substantial evidence against him, Ray insisted that he had not killed King, and that the assassination was the work of a mysterious conspiracy in which he was only minimally involved. His lies deceived Dr. King's family, and one of King's sons visited Ray in prison, told him he believed him, and shook his hand. A disturbing photograph of their meeting depicts a reluctant Ray with his hands at his side, staring uncomfortably at the young Dexter King's extended hand.

Ray gave interviews and wrote a book. Until the end, he denied that he was the assassin. James Earl Ray died on April 23, 1998. He

James Earl Ray spent the rest of his life in prison.

was seventy years old, and he had outlived Martin Luther King by thirty years.

Ralph David Abernathy continued the good work of the civil rights movement. In 1989, he published his splendid autobiography, *And the Walls Came Tumbling Down.* No man had spent more time with Martin Luther King, knew him better, or loved him more. But Abernathy was criticized unfairly for portraying his old friend not falsely as a perfect saint but truthfully as a human being. Sadly, Abernathy died the next year, in 1990, at age sixty-four. He deserved more time, the kind of long life that his friend Martin had spoken about on April 3, 1968.

After King's assassination, Coretta Scott King continued his work and helped lead the civil rights movement. She believed that women had important contributions to make. "Not enough attention," she once said, "had been focused on the roles played by women in the struggle . . . women have been at the backbone of the whole civil rights movement." In 1969, she published her memoirs, *My Life with Martin Luther King, Jr.*, when her recollections were still fresh and her pain was raw; her account of Martin's death was heartbreaking. When former president Johnson died in 1973, Coretta attended his funeral—it was out of respect for the man who had once made history with her husband. She worked to have Martin's birthday made the national holiday it is today. Coretta lived a full and active life, and she never remarried. She died in January 2006 at the age of seventy-eight. She had survived her husband by thirty-eight years.

Finally, in March 2015, a frail, forgotten, ninety-eight-year-old woman died at a nursing home in the Bronx, in New York City. She had been in the custody of mental institutions and care centers for decades. No friends or family ever came to visit her. Most people assumed she had died a long time ago. A journalist who found her shortly before her death learned that she had no recollection of the notorious event that had once made her infamous. Her conversation made little sense, but she had outlived them all. History had passed Izola Ware Curry by, for few people remembered how, fifty-seven years earlier on a fall day in Harlem, she had tried to assassinate Dr. Martin Luther King, Jr., and had almost ended this story before it ever began.

In the end, an assassin's bullet could never erase what Martin Luther King achieved, or the legacy he created. But his death left behind a void. Jacqueline Kennedy, speaking of her murdered husband, once said, "Every man can make a difference, and every man should try."

During his short life, Martin Luther King had tried to make a difference and he changed history. What else might he have accomplished if he had been around to help lead the civil rights movement into the 1970s, 1980s, or even today? Abraham Lincoln once spoke of his own "unfinished work." If he had not been assassinated and had lived to heal the nation after the Civil War, America would have been a better place.

Like Lincoln, Martin Luther King summoned the nation to fulfill its promise of equal rights to all citizens. King's all-too-brief life left much of his work undone, and his time was cut short before he could fulfill his potential. He was just thirty-nine years old, such a young man.

This photo was taken on April 3, 1968, the last full day of King's life, and the day before he was shot.

Today, Dr. Martin Luther King, Jr., is admired around the world as a great hero of our time. We can look back and speculate, but we will never know the ways in which his death altered the future course of American history. Yet we can be sure of one thing. Because of him, America is a better place, though still not fully what King hoped for and worked so hard to achieve.

He knew such changes would not come easily. King was all too aware of the sacrifices required. As he said prophetically in his last speech, "I may not get there with you. But I want you to know tonight, that we, as a people, will get to the Promised Land." He had so many dreams. But he did not live to see them all come true.

And so King might ask us: Where do we go from here? How long will it take?

How long?

The spirit of the civil rights movement and of Dr. Martin Luther King, Jr., live on in many places, and there is no better time to visit them. We are at the dawn of civil rights tourism. Just as Americans visit the battlefields of the American Revolution and the Civil War, or the homes of the presidents like George Washington's Mount Vernon, Thomas Jefferson's Monticello, or Abraham Lincoln's modest frame house in Springfield, Illinois, the nation's civil rights landmarks draw increasing numbers of visitors every year.

In Washington, DC, at the Smithsonian National Museum of American History, you can visit a section of the famous lunch counter at the Woolworth's Store in Greensboro, North Carolina, where four black college students were denied service when they refused to give up their seats and helped change history. This iconic relic looks just as it did on February 1, 1960, when it became the center of national attention. At the Lincoln Memorial, you can climb the stairs and stand on the exact spot where, during the March on Washington on August 28, 1963, Martin Luther King gave his "I Have a Dream" speech. A stone block marks the spot. From there you can face the Washington Monument and enjoy the same view that Dr. King did on that historic day—and imagine the sea of hundreds of thousands of faces looking up and waiting for him and other key leaders to speak.

The Newseum on Pennsylvania Avenue has a fine exhibit on civil rights history that highlights not only Dr. King but also the other important leaders of the movement, and which includes the iron-barred door to the cell where King wrote his famous "Letter from Birmingham Jail." You can visit the Martin Luther King monument and the new Smithsonian National Museum of African American History and Culture, which includes exhibits on the history of the civil rights movement.

In Birmingham, Alabama, the Sixteenth Street Baptist Church is a moving place of quiet pilgrimage. It was here, on September 15, 1963, that a bomb exploded during Sunday school, killing four little girls. The edifice serves as both a church and a museum where a clock, its hands still frozen in place, forever marks the time of the explosion. A visitor can stand on the very spot where the bomb blasted a hole through the brick wall of the church, and I remain haunted by my time there. It is easy to imagine the voice of Martin Luther King still echoing inside the church from the day he bade farewell to the "sweet princesses" who lost their lives there. In a striking juxtaposition, in a public park a few blocks away, a Confederate obelisk stands alongside monuments from America's other wars.

In Atlanta, Martin Luther King's home still stands, as does the spiritual and physical center of his ministry, Ebenezer Baptist Church.

Also in Atlanta is the Martin Luther King, Jr. Center for Nonviolent Social Change, and it is there that he and his wife, Coretta Scott King, are buried.

In New York City, in Harlem, Blumstein's department store, the place where Izola Curry attempted to end King's life in 1958, closed long ago, but the building still stands as a ghostly landmark to an episode in King's life that has been mostly forgotten.

In Memphis, Tennessee, the Lorraine Motel still stands, its famous colorful sign still inviting visitors. The Lorraine no longer accommodates overnight guests, but instead beckons daytime tourists on the civil rights trail. Like Ford's Theatre in Washington, DC, and the Texas School Book Depository in Dallas, Texas, it is appropriate that the Lorraine has become a place of pilgrimage where Americans honor an assassinated hero. Today it is home to the National Civil Rights Museum. Once, some people wanted to tear down the Lorraine as an ugly reminder of a terrible tragedy. But more visionary voices prevailed, and it was preserved for history, and today teaches the lessons of the past to future generations.

It is easy to overlook the history right in front of our eyes. The history of the civil rights movement is all around you, in the living memories of those who participated in it. Many people alive today saw Martin Luther King, Jr., in person, or even met him. Some knew him well. Did anyone in your family participate in the civil rights movement? Ask your grandparents and great-grandparents, your aunts and uncles, and old family friends to share their recollections of those times. What was it like to be part of a great social movement? Where were they the day they learned that Martin Luther King was dead? In basements and attics all across America, perhaps even in your own home, documents and relics from the movement—picket signs, posters, photographs, souvenirs, event programs, pin-back buttons, and more—have been hidden away for decades. These things should be rediscovered, cherished, and preserved. Interview family members and friends, or ask them to write down their recollections. History dies forever unless those living today work to pass it on to future generations.

First bill introduced in the U.S. House of Representatives four days after King's death in 1968 by Rep. John Conyers (D-MI).

96TH CONGRESS (1979-1980)

U.S. Senate. *Martin Luther King, Jr., National Holiday Bill* (S. 25). Joint Hearings before the Senate Judiciary Committee, the House Post Office and Civil Service Committee. 96th Congress, 1st Session, March 27 and June 21, 1979. Washington, DC: Government Printing Office, 1979.

S.25, a bill to designate the birthday of Martin Luther King Junior a legal public holiday. Reported to the Senate from the Committee on Judiciary, Senate Report 96-284, August 1, 1979.

H.R. 5461, a bill to designate the birthday of Martin Luther King, Jr., a legal public holiday. Reported from the House Post Office and Civil Service Committee, House Report 97-543, October 23, 1979.

H.R. 5461, failed passage in the House of Representatives under suspension of the rules, 252 ayes to 133 noes, November 13, 1979.

97TH CONGRESS (1981-1982)

U.S. House of Representatives. *Martin Luther King, Jr., Holiday Bill.* (H.R. 800). Hearings before the Subcommittee on Census and Population of the House Post Office and Civil Service Committee. 97th Congress, 2nd Session, February 23, 1982. Washington, DC: Government Printing Office, 1982.

98TH CONGRESS (1983-1984)

U.S. House of Representatives. *Martin Luther King, Jr., Holiday Bill.* (H.R. 800) Hearings before the Subcommittee on Census and Statistics of the House Post Office and Civil Service Committee. 98th Congress, 1st Session. June 7, 1983. Washington, DC: Government Printing Office, 1983.

H.R. 3345, as reported to the House of Representatives. House Report 98-314 on July 26, 1983.

H.R. 3706, as passed by the House of Representatives under suspension of the rules, by a vote of 338 ayes to 90 noes on August 2, 1983, and as passed by the Senate by a vote of 78 ayes to 22 noes on October 19, 1983.

Public Law 98-144, signed by President Reagan on November 2, 1983. (Observance every third Monday in January, beginning 1986.)

Creation of the Martin Luther King, Jr., Holiday Commission. Public Law 98-399 (transferred to the King Center in 1996).

November 18, 1948—Charged with the violation of the 96th Article of War (being drunk in quarters on October 31), and charged with the violation of the 69th Article of War (and after being duly placed under arrest on November 3 for breaking arrest before he was set "at liberty"). Sentenced to hard labor for three months at the stockade at Nuremberg, and forfeiture of his pay ($45 per month for four months).

December 10, 1948—Hard labor sentenced was commuted and Ray returned to the United States.

December 23, 1948—Discharged for "ineptness." (After thirty-four months and four days in uniform—never obtaining the rank higher than private first class).

December 9, 1949—Convicted of second degree burglary in Los Angeles, California (sentenced to eight months in county jail and two-year probation).

March 1950—Application for early release approved.

April 1950—Jailed in Cedar Rapids, Iowa, for suspicion of robbery and vagrancy, but released.

July 23, 1951—Jailed in Alton, Illinois, for vagrancy and given ninety-day sentence.

June 4, 1952—Sentenced to one to two years and sent to Joliet State Penitentiary after having pled guilty to armed robbery of a taxi driver in Chicago, Illinois.

Early July 1952—Transferred to the state penitentiary at Pontiac.

March 12, 1954—Released after serving twenty-two months of his sentence.

August 28, 1954—Arrested for suspicion of numerous petty crimes in Alton, Illinois. Posted bail and skipped town.

April 1955—Convicted in Kansas City, Missouri, for mail fraud and stealing money orders, in Hannibal, Missouri. Received forty-five-month sentence.

July 7, 1955—Arrived at Leavenworth prison.

April 5, 1958—Released from "honor" farm where he resided for about one year.

October 10, 1959—Committed armed robbery of a few Kroger grocery stores in St. Louis, Missouri.

October 26, 1959—Found guilty of armed robbery on parole, so sentenced to twenty years for repeated offenses.

March 17, 1960—Transferred from the city jail to the Missouri State Penitentiary.

April 23, 1967—Escaped from Missouri State Penitentiary by hiding in a breadbox in a truck transporting bread to prison bakery.

POST-ASSASSINATION

June 8, 1968—Captured at London Heathrow Airport.

March 10, 1969—Pled guilty, sentenced to ninety-nine years in prison.

May 3, 1971—Attempted escape through ventilation fan and manhole on a steam tunnel that led to the outside of prison wall, after placing a dummy in his bed. It was too hot in the tunnel, so he returned to the prison yard.

February 1972—Attempted escape by cutting a hole through the ceiling in his work area.

June 10, 1977—Escaped from Brushy Mountain State Prison with six other inmates, using a pipe ladder over the fourteen-foot back wall.

June 13, 1977—Recaptured, and two years was added to his ninety-nine-year sentence.

November 9, 1979—Attempted escape but captured when a guard caught him crawling along the base of the prison wall under a camouflage blanket.

June 4, 1981—Stabbed twenty-two times in prison library by four inmates, three black and one white. Required seventy-seven stitches.

December 1996–April 1998—Hospitalized more than a dozen times.

April 23, 1998—Ray died in prison from kidney and liver disease.

(The principal sources for this chronology are McMillan, *Making of an Assassin*; Posner, *Killing the Dream*; Sides, *Hellhound on His Trail*; U.S. House Select Committee on Assassinations [Final Report and Appendixes]; and various *New York Times* articles.)

PROLOGUE: "A SNEEZE MEANT DEATH"

The stabbing of King by Izola Curry. While King had received national attention with brief stories in the *New York Times* and the *Wall Street Journal,* the most complete coverage of the events surrounding the stabbing was in the weekly black newspaper the *New York Amsterdam News,* September 27, 1958, and, to a lesser extent, in the *Chicago Defender,* September 27, 1958, another influential weekly for African American readers. See also the graphic photographic coverage in the *Sunday News: New York's Picture Newspaper,* "Martin Luther King Stabbed," September 21, 1958. In addition, see Hugh Pearson, *When Harlem Nearly Killed King: The 1958 Stabbing of Dr. Martin Luther King, Jr.* (New York: Seven Stories Press, 2002), and go to: http://www.thesmokinggun.com /documents/crime/the-woman-who-nearly-murdered-martin -luther-king-jr-687453. In addition, see King's comments about this incident at: http://kingencyclopedia.stanford.edu/encyclopedia /documentsentry/from_dexter_avenue_baptist_church_21 _sept_1958/index.html and http://kingencyclopedia.stanford.edu /encyclopedia/documentsentry/statement_upon_return_to _montgomery/index.html, and additional material, as found in *The Papers of Martin Luther King, Jr.: Volume IV, Symbol of the*

Movement, January 1957–December 1958 (Berkeley: University of California Press, 2000, including King's full statement from Harlem Hospital), 502, and 513–514.

PART ONE: INTRODUCTION TO MARTIN LUTHER KING, JR., AND THE CIVIL RIGHTS MOVEMENT

1865-1958: JIM CROW AMERICA

Overview. I must pay tribute to my mentor and friend, the late John Hope Franklin. The most updated edition of his seminal work remains a classic: John Hope Franklin and Evelyn Higginbotham, *From Slavery to Freedom: A History of African Americans*, 9th ed. (New York: McGraw-Hill, 2010).

Jim Crow. See C. Vann Woodward, *Strange Career of Jim Crow* (New York: Oxford University Press, 1955). Also, William H. Chafe, et al. *Remembering Jim Crow: African Americans Tell About Life in the Segregated South* (New York: The New Press, 2001).

Ku Klux Klan (KKK). See David M. Chalmers, *Hooded Americanism: The First Century of the Ku Klux Klan, 1865–1965* (Garden City: Doubleday & Co., 1965), and updated as *Hooded Americanism: The History of the Ku Klux Klan* (Durham: Duke University

Press, 1987). Also, Elaine Frantz Parsons, *Ku-Klux: The Birth of the Klan during Reconstruction* (Chapel Hill: The University of North Carolina Press, 2015) and William Rawlings, *The Second Coming of the Invisible Empire: The Ku Klux Klan of the 1920s* (Macon: Mercer University Press, 2016).

Lynching. *Lynching in America: Confronting the Legacy of Racial Terror*, 2nd ed. (Montgomery, AL: Equal Justice Initiative, 2015), http://eji.org /sites/default/files/lynching-in-america-second-edition-summary .pdf; James Allen, *Without Sanctuary: Lynching Photography in America* (Santa Fe, NM: Twin Palms Press, 2000); Christopher Waldrep, *Lynching in America: A History in Documents* (New York: New York University Press, 2006); and Philip Dray, *At the Hands of Persons Unknown: The Lynching of Black America* (New York: Random House, 2002).

THE EARLY YEARS

King's early years and biography. An appropriate place to begin is the edited work by Clayborne Carson, ed., *The Autobiography of Martin Luther King, Jr.* (New York: Warner Books, 1998). See also Marshall Frady, *Martin Luther King, Jr.: A Life.* (New York: Penguin Group, 2002); Lerone Bennett, Jr., *What Manner of Man: A Biography of Martin Luther King, Jr.*, 4th revised edition (Chicago: Johnson Publishing, 1964, 1976); Lawrence D. Reddick, *Crusader without Violence: A Biography of Martin Luther King, Jr.* (New York: Harper and Brothers, 1959); and Stephen Oates, *Let the Trumpet Sound: The Life of Martin Luther King, Jr.* (New York: Harper & Row, 1982).

The birth name of Martin Luther King, Jr., was Michael—the same as his father. As a pastor, his father traveled to Berlin, Germany, to attend the Fifth Baptist World Alliance Conference, and inspired by the Protestant Reformation leader, Martin Luther, he subsequently renamed himself and his five-year-old son.

The Montgomery bus boycott. Important firsthand accounts include King's own book, *Stride Toward Freedom: A Leader of His People Tells the Montgomery Story* (New York: Harper & Row, 1958), as well as Uriah J. Fields, *Inside the Montgomery Bus Boycott: My Personal Story* (Baltimore: America House, 2002); Fred D. Gray, *Bus Ride to Freedom: The Life and Works of Fred Gray* (Montgomery: Black Belt Press, 1995); Rosa Parks and Jim Haskins, *Rosa Parks: My Story* (New York: Dial Books, 1992); and Jo Ann Robinson (edited by David J. Garrow), *The Montgomery Bus Boycott and the Women Who Started It: The Memoir of Jo Ann Gibson Robinson* (Knoxville: University of Tennessee Press, 1987). Additionally, see David J. Garrow, ed., *The Walking City: The Montgomery Bus Boycott, 1955–1956* (Brooklyn: Carlson Publishing, 1969); Willy S. Leventhal, *The Children Coming On: A Retrospective of the Montgomery Bus Boycott* (Montgomery, AL: Black Belt Press, 1968); Stewart Burns, ed., *Daybreak of Freedom: The Montgomery Bus Boycott* (Chapel Hill: University of North Carolina Press, 1997); and Donnie Williams and Wayne Greenhaw, *The Thunder of Angels: The Montgomery Bus Boycott and the People Who Broke the Back of Jim Crow* (Chicago: Lawrence Hill Books, 2006).

The civil rights movement. The literature on this subject is rich with personal memoirs of participants, and also with critical scholarly works, as noted in my selected bibliography. An ideal place to begin is with Taylor Branch's monumental trilogy on this topic. See Taylor Branch, *Parting the Waters: America in the King Years, 1954–1963* (New York: Simon & Schuster, 1989); *Pillar of Fire: America in the King Years, 1963–1965* (New York: Simon & Schuster, 1998); *At Canaan's Edge: America in the King Years, 1965–1968* (New York: Simon & Schuster, 2006). See also David Garrow, *Bearing the Cross: Martin Luther King, Jr., and the Southern Christian Leadership Conference* (New York: William Morrow, 1986). And for President Lyndon Johnson's response leading up to the signing of the Civil Rights Act, see Brian A. McKee, et al., eds., *The Presidential Recordings; Lyndon B. Johnson: Mississippi Burning and the Passage of the Civil Rights Act, June 1, 1964–July 4, 1964,* Volumes 7 and 8 (New York: W. W. Norton & Company, 2011).

Climate of violence against King and the civil rights movement. Between 1955 and 1965, Martin Luther King, Jr., was arrested thirty times—largely for his nonviolence protest activities, as well as "trumped-up" charges, such as driving five miles over the speed limit. Similar to many others in the civil rights movement, King's life—as well as his family's—was constantly in danger wherever he appeared. Besides the bomb threats and other physical dangers, there was an explosion at his home in Montgomery in January 1956, and in months afterward as well. So it should come as no surprise that there were guns in his home, and a few of his associates carried weapons. Some may see an irony in King's nonviolent philosophy and the perceived need to be armed. But the history and use of arms in the black community, including during the 1960s, is a fascinating one. See Charles E. Cobb, Jr., *This Nonviolent Stuff'll Get You Killed: How Guns Made the Civil Rights Movement Possible* (New York: Basic Books, 2015); Nicholas Johnson, *Negroes and the Gun: The Black Tradition of Arms* (Amherst: Prometheus Books, 2014), 209–284 (Chapter Seven, "Freedom Fight"); and Simon Wendt, *The Spirit and the Shotgun: Armed Resistance and the Struggle for Civil Rights* (Gainesville: University Press of Florida, 2007).

Brown v. Board of Education. For the complete text of the U.S. Supreme Court decision, see *Brown v. Board of Education*, 347 U.S. 483 (1954), https://www.law.cornell.edu/supremecourt/text/347/483. Also, see Leon Friedman, ed., *Argument: The Oral Argument Before the Supreme Court in Brown v. Board of Education of Topeka 1952–1955* (New York: Chelsea House, 1983); Jack Greenberg, *Brown v. Board of Education: Witness to a Landmark Decision*, 50th Anniversary Edition (New York: Twelve Tables Press, 2004); Richard Kluger, *Simple Justice: The History of Brown v. Board of Education and Black America's Struggle for Equality* (New York: Alfred A. Knopf, 1976); Waldo E. Martin, Jr., *Brown v. Board of Education: A Brief History with Documents* (Boston: Bedford/St. Martin's Press, 1998); James T. Patterson, Brown v. Board of Education: *A Civil Rights Milestone and Its Troubled Legacy* (New York: Oxford University Press, 2001);

and Paul E. Wilson, *A Time to Lose: Representing Kansas in Brown v. Board of Education* (Lawrence: University Press of Kansas, 1995).

1959-1962: ON THE RISE: LUNCH COUNTERS, FREEDOM RIDERS, AND OLE MISS

Lunch counters. For instance, see Miles Wolff, *Lunch at the Five and Ten: The Greensboro Sit-ins* (New York: Stein and Day, 1970); Merrill Proudfoot, *Diary of a Sit-In* (Chapel Hill: University of North Carolina Press, 1962); and William Chafe, *Civilities and Civil Rights: Greensboro, North Carolina, and the Black Struggle for Freedom* (New York: Oxford University Press, 1980).

Freedom Riders. See Raymond Arsenault, *Freedom Riders: 1961 and the Struggle for Racial Justice* (New York: Oxford University Press, 2006) and PBS, *American Experience: Freedom Riders*, 2001 (DVD). See also Eric Etheridge and Roger Wilkens, *Breach of Peace: Portraits of the 1961 Freedom Riders* (New York: Atlas & Co., 2008).

Ole Miss. The most important primary source was written by the first black student to enroll at the University of Mississippi: James Meredith, *Three Years in Mississippi* (Bloomington: Indiana University Press, 1966). See also Henry T. Gallagher, *James Meredith and the Ole Miss Riot: A Soldier's Story* (Jackson: University Press of Mississippi, 2012) and Charles W. Eagles, *The Price of Defiance: James Meredith and the Integration of Ole Miss* (Chapel Hill: University of North Carolina Press, 2009).

1963: TRAGEDIES AND TRIUMPHS: PROTESTS IN BIRMINGHAM, A LETTER FROM JAIL, AND A MARCH ON WASHINGTON

Letter from Birmingham Jail. This letter originally was published by the American Friends Service Committee as a small stapled pamphlet in May 1963. See also Jonathan Rieder, *Gospel of Freedom: Martin Luther King, Jr.'s Letter from Birmingham Jail and the Struggle That Changed a Nation* (New York: Bloomsbury Press, 2013). To view the letter and hear King read his words, go to: https://kinginstitute .stanford.edu/king-papers/documents/letter-birmingham-jail

The March on Washington and the "I Have a Dream" speech. See Clarence Jones, *Behind the Dream: The Making of a Speech That Transformed a Nation* (New York: Palgrave Macmillan, 2011) and William P. Jones, *March on Washington: Jobs, Freedom and the Forgotten History of the Civil Rights Movement* (New York: W. W. Norton & Co., 2013). Also, see generally, Charles Euchner, *Nobody Turn Me Around: A People's History of the 1963 March on Washington* (Boston: Beacon Press, 2010); Thomas Gentile, *March on Washington, August 28, 1963* (Washington, DC: New Day Publications, 1983); Leonard Freed (photographer), *This Is the Day: The March on Washington* (Los Angeles: The J. Paul Getty Museum, 2013); and Kitty Kelly, *Let Freedom Ring: Stanley Tretlick's Iconic Images of the March on Washington* (New York: St. Martin's Press, 2013). Also go to: http:// kingencyclopedia.stanford.edu/encyclopedia/encyclopedia/enc _march_on_washington_for_jobs_and_freedom/index.html. For the complete text of King's speech, go to:

http://kingencyclopedia.stanford.edu/kingweb/publications/speeches
/address_at_march_on_washington.pdf and Clayborne Carson and
Kris Shepard, eds., *A Call to Conscience: the Landmark Speeches of
Dr. Martin Luther King, Jr.* (New York: IPM [Intellectual Properties
Management] in association with Warner Books, 2001), 75–88.

King's sermons and speeches. All further quotations in this book on
the speeches of Martin Luther King, Jr., are found in the following sources: The King Paper Project at Stanford University has already
published seven volumes containing correspondence, sermons,
speeches, published writing, and unpublished manuscripts. Much
material is available online at: https://kinginstitute.stanford.edu/ and
https://kinginstitute.stanford.edu/king-papers/about-papers-project

Murder of Medgar Evers. See Adam Nossiter, *Of Long Memory:
Mississippi and the Murder of Medgar Evers* (Reading, MA: Addison
Wesley, 1994).

1963: DISASTER AND HOPE: A BOMBING IN BIRMING-HAM, THE ASSASSINATION OF A PRESIDENT, AND A NEW LEADER

The Sixteenth Street Baptist Church bombing. This, the oldest
black church in Birmingham, was first organized in 1873. For a brief
description of its history, see http://16thstreetbaptist.org/history-2/.
See also Elizabeth H. Cobbs and Petric J. Smith, *Long Time
Coming: An Insider's Story of the Birmingham Church Bombing
That Rocked the World* (Birmingham: Crane Hill, 1994); Frank

Sikora, *Until Justice Rolls Down: The Birmingham Church Bombing Case* (Tuscaloosa: University of Alabama Press, 1991); and T. K. Thorne, *Last Chance for Justice: How Relentless Investigators Uncovered New Evidence Convicting the Birmingham Church Bombers* (Chicago: Lawrence Hill Books, 2013). See also the FBI vault website: https://vault.fbi.gov/16th%20Street%20Church%20Bombing %20 (in 50 parts).

For the text of King's eulogy for three of the four children killed in the bombing (there was a separate service for the fourth victim), see Carson, *A Call to Conscience*, 89–100.

Assassination of John F. Kennedy. For a thorough treatment of the JFK assassination, see James L. Swanson, *"The President Has Been Shot!": The Assassination of John F. Kennedy* (New York: Scholastic Press, 2013) and James L. Swanson, *End of Days: The Assassination of John F. Kennedy* (New York: HarperCollins Publishers, 2013).

1964: FROM THE CIVIL RIGHTS BILL AND THE NOBEL PRIZE TO A MURDER AND A SLANDER

The Civil Rights Act. This landmark legislation was signed into Public Law by President Lyndon Johnson on July 2, 1964 (Public Law 88-352), https://www.ourdocuments.gov/doc.php?doc=97& page=transcript. See also Clay Risen, *The Bill of the Century: The Epic Battle for the Civil Rights Act* (New York: Bloomsbury Press, 2014); Todd S. Purdum, *An Idea Whose Time Had Come: Two Presidents, Two Parties, and the Battle for the Civil Rights Act of 1964* (New York:

Henry Holt & Co., 1964); Charles Whalen, *The Longest Debate: A Legislative History of the 1964 Civil Rights Act* (Washington, DC: Seven Locks Press, 1985); and https://www.loc.gov/exhibits/civil-rights-act/civil-rights-act-of-1964.html

Mississippi burning (killing of the three civil rights workers). See William Bradford Huie, *Three Lives for Mississippi*, 2nd edition with introduction by Dr. Martin Luther King, Jr. (New York: New American Library, 1968); Seth Cagin and Phillip Drey, *We Are Not Afraid: The Story of Goodman, Schwerner, and Chaney and the Civil Rights Campaign for Mississippi* (New York: Macmillan Publishing, 1988); Bruce Watson, *Freedom Summer: The Savage Season of 1964 That Made Mississippi Burn and Made America a Democracy* (New York: Viking Press, 2010); and Howard Ball, *Murder in Mississippi: United States v. Price and the Struggle for Civil Rights* (Lawrence: University Press of Kansas, 2004), and *Justice in Mississippi: The Murder Trial of Edgar Ray Killen* (Lawrence: University Press of Kansas, 2008). See also the FBI vault website: https://vault.fbi.gov/Mississippi%20Burning%20(MIBURN)%20Case (in 9 parts), and U.S. Department of Justice Report to the Attorney General of the State of Mississippi, *Investigation of the 1964 Murders of Michael Schwerner, James Chaney, and Andrew Goodman* (Washington, DC: U.S. Department of Justice, Civil Rights Division, 2016), http://www.ago.state.ms.us/wp-content/uploads/2016/06/DOJ-Report-to-Mississippi-Attorney-General-Jim-Hood.pdf

The Department of Justice finally closed the investigation of this case in June 2016.

The FBI suicide letter. For the text of the letter, see Beverly Gage, "What an Uncensored Letter to M.L.K. Reveals," *New York Times,* November 11, 2014, http://www.nytimes.com/2014/11/16/magazine /what-an-uncensored-letter-to-mlk-reveals.html

For a scholarly treatment of the harassment activities of the FBI against King, see David J. Garrow, *The FBI and Martin Luther King, Jr., from "Solo" to Memphis* (New York: W. W. Norton, 1981).

The Nobel Peace Prize. To see a video of King's acceptance speech, go to: http://www.nobelprize.org/nobel_prizes/peace/laureates /1964/king-acceptance.html. For the complete text, go to: http:// kingencyclopedia.stanford.edu/encyclopedia/documentsentry/doc _acceptance_speech_at_nobel_peace_prize_ceremony/index.html and see Carson, *Call to Conscience,* 101–110.

1965: NEW CHALLENGES AND WARNING SIGNS: THE ASSASSINATION OF MALCOLM X, THE BATTLE FOR SELMA, THE VOTING RIGHTS ACT, AND THE WATTS RIOTS

Assassination of Malcolm X. Most of the works published on this assassination propound conspiratorial motifs with nefarious involvement of the New York Police Department, the FBI, the CIA, and even Louis Farrakhan (the current leader of the Nation of

Islam). Malcolm X's family supports this latter allegation. See Karl Evanzz, *The Judas Factor: The Plot to Kill Malcolm X* (Emeryville: Thunder's Mouth Press, 1992), and George Breitman, Herman Porter, and Baxter Smith, *The Assassination of Malcom X* (New York: Pathfinder's Press, 1976). For an overview of Malcolm X's life, see Malcolm X, *The Autobiography of Malcolm X, as told to Alex Haley* (New York: Grove Press, 1966) and Peter Goldman, *The Death and Life of Malcolm X* (New York: Harper & Row, 1973).

Selma. For a firsthand account, see John Lewis and Michael D'Orso, *Walking with the Wind: A Memoir of the Movement* (New York: Simon & Schuster, 1998). Also visit the websites of the National Voting Museum and Institute in Selma at: http://nvrmi.com/, and the National Park Service Trail at http://www.nps.gov/nr/travel /civilrights/al4.htm. See also David J. Garrow, *Protest at Selma: Martin Luther King, Jr., and the Voting Rights Act of 1965* (New Haven, CT: Yale University Press, 1978); Thornton J. Mills III, *Dividing Lines: Municipal Politics and the Struggle for Civil Rights in Montgomery and Selma* (Tuscaloosa: University of Alabama Press, 2002); and for the text of King's "On the Move" speech at the end of the march, go to: http://kingencyclopedia.stanford.edu/encyclopedia/documentsentry /doc_address_at_the_conclusion_of_selma_march/, and Carson, *Call to Conscience*, 111–132.

The Voting Rights Act. This monumental statute was signed into Public Law by President Lyndon Johnson on August 6, 1965 (Public Law 89-110). See https://ourdocuments.gov/doc.php?flash=true&

doc=100. For the events leading up to the passage of this legislation, see the second volume of Taylor Branch's trilogy, *Pillar of Fire*. And to put this legislation into the historical and legal significance of the advancement of American democracy, see Gary May, *Bending toward Justice: The Voting Rights Act and the Transformation of American Democracy* (Durham: Duke University Press, 2014); Richard M. Valelly, ed., *The Voting Rights Act: Securing the Ballot* (Washington, DC: CQ Press, 2005); and Chandler Davison and Bernard Grofman, eds., *Quiet Revolution in the South: The Impact of the Voting Rights Act, 1965–1990* (Princeton: Princeton University Press, 1994).

Watts riot. See Jerry Cohen and William S. Murphy, *Burn, Baby, Burn! The Los Angeles Race Riot, August 1965* (New York: Dutton, 1966); Gerald Horne, *Fire This Time: The Watts Uprising and the 1960s* (Charlottesville: University of Virginia Press, 1995); and David O. Sears and John B. McConahay, *The Politics of Violence: The New Urban Blacks and the Watts Riot* (Boston: Houghton Mifflin, 1973).

1966: A YEAR OF DOUBTS AND DIVISIONS: CHICAGO, BLACK PANTHERS, AND MILITANTS

King in Chicago. See Andrew Young, *An Easy Burden: The Civil Rights Movement and the Transformation of America* (New York: HarperCollins Publishers, 1996), Chapter 13, "Going to Chicago"; David J. Garrow, *Bearing the Cross: Martin Luther King, Jr., and the Southern Christian Leadership Conference* (New York: William Morrow, 1986), Chapter 8, "Chicago and the 'War on Slums,' 1965–1966; James R. Ralph, *Northern Protest: Martin Luther King, Jr.,*

Chicago and the Civil Rights Movement (Cambridge: Harvard University Press, 1993); and Alan B. Anderson and George W. Pickering, *Confronting the Color Line: The Broken Promise of the Civil Rights Movement in Chicago* (Athens: University of Georgia Press, 1986).

The radical black movement vs. King's nonviolence approach. While the Southern Christian Leadership Conference (SCLC) and its leader, Dr. Martin Luther King, Jr., were central and pivotal forces, the civil rights movement was not a monolithic entity. There were several other organizations, such as the Black Panthers and the Black Muslims. They advocated a more confrontational, and even violent approach, to gain civil rights for African Americans, who had seen little progress in more than a century, since the end of the Civil War. Even within the SCLC, there was a great diversity of opinion as to how to best proceed to achieve success.

1967: SPLITTING THE MOVEMENT AND OPPOSITION TO THE VIETNAM WAR

King, LBJ, and Vietnam. See Nick Kotz, *Judgment Days: Lyndon Baines Johnson, Martin Luther King Jr., and the Laws That Changed History* (Boston: Houghton Mifflin, 2005). For the text of King's "Beyond Vietnam: A Time to Break the Silence" speech of April 4, 1967, go to: http://kingencyclopedia.stanford.edu/encyclopedia/documentsentry /doc_beyond_vietnam/, and Carson, *Call to Conscience*, 133–164. To listen to the audio of most of the speech, go to: https://archive.org /details/MartinLutherKing-BeyondVietnam-1967. For the text of King's "Why I Am Opposed to the War in Vietnam" sermon of April

30, 1967, at the Riverside Church in New York, go to: http://www.lib .berkeley.edu/MRC/pacificaviet/riversidetranscript.html

See also Garrow, *Bearing the Cross*, Chapter 10, "Economic Justice and Vietnam, 1966–1967," 527–574.

PART TWO: A COLLISION COURSE

APRIL 23, 1967: A JAIL BREAK

Ray's early life, military service, crimes, and prison escape. Two important indispensable early works are: Gerold Frank, *An American Death: The True Story of the Assassination of Dr. Martin Luther King, Jr. and the Greatest Manhunt of Our Time* (Garden City: Doubleday, 1972), and William Bradford Huie, *He Slew the Dreamer: My Search for the Truth about James Earl Ray and the Murder of Martin Luther King* (New York: Delacorte Press, 1970). For an insightful examination of the psychology of Ray, see George McMillan, *The Making of an Assassin: The Life of James Earl Ray* (Boston: Little, Brown, 1976). The two most comprehensive works on James Earl Ray and the assassination of Martin Luther King are Gerald L. Posner, *Killing the Dream: James Earl Ray and the Assassination of Martin Luther King, Jr.* (New York: Random House, 1998), and Hampton Sides, *Hellhound on His Trail: The Stalking of Martin Luther King, Jr. and the International Hunt for His Assassin* (New York: Doubleday, 2010).

1968: A VERY BAD YEAR

The Memphis Sanitation Workers Strike. For a photographic history of this incident, see D'Army Bailey, *Mine Eyes Have Seen: Dr. Martin Luther King Jr.'s Final Journey* (Memphis: Towery Publishing, 1993) and Jeff McAdory, ed., *I Am a Man: Photographs of the 1968 Memphis Sanitation Strike and Dr. Martin Luther King Jr.* (Memphis: Memphis Publishing, 1993). Also for a comprehensive overview, see Michael K. Honey, *Going Down Jericho Road: The Memphis Strike, Martin Luther King's Last Campaign* (New York: W. W. Norton, 2007); and for an important primary source account, see Joan Turner Beifuss, *At the River I Stand: Memphis, the 1968 Strike, and Martin Luther King* (Brooklyn: Carlson Publishing, 1989).

PART THREE: THE ASSASSINATION

PLANNING A MURDER

Ray's activities. The most comprehensive works on this subject are Posner, *Killing the Dream* and Sides, *Hellhound on His Trail*, and the earlier work, Huie, *He Slew the Dreamer*.

King's activities and his relationship with Ralph Abernathy, SCLC, and the final days in Memphis. See Ralph David Abernathy, *And the Walls Came Tumbling Down: An Autobiography* (New York: Harper & Row, 1989), 412–493. Also, for firsthand accounts of King's activities in the final days, see Andrew Young, *An Easy*

Burden: The Civil Rights Movement and the Transformation of America (New York: HarperCollins Publishers, 1996), Chapter 16, "Let Us Slay the Dreamer."

MARCH 31, 1968: MOMENTOUS DAYS

LBJ's decision to not seek reelection. See *Public Papers of the Presidents of the United States: Lyndon B. Johnson, 1968–69, Book 1* (Washington, DC: Government Printing Office, 1970), 469–476. http://www.lbjlib.utexas.edu/johnson/archives.hom/speeches.hom /680331.asp

See also Horace W. Busby, *The Thirty-First of March: An Intimate Portrait of Lyndon Johnson's Final Days in Office* (New York: Farrar, Straus and Giroux, 2005); George Christian, *The President Steps Down: A Personal Memoir of the Transfer of Power* (New York: Macmillan, 1970); Herbert Y. Schander, *The Unmaking of a President: Lyndon Johnson and Vietnam* (Princeton: Princeton University Press, 1977); and Robert Dallek, *Flawed Giant: Lyndon Johnson and His Times, 1961–1975* (New York: Oxford University Press, 1998), 519–530.

APRIL 1 AND 2, 1968: COUNTDOWN TO MEMPHIS

King's and Ray's movements. As sourced above.

APRIL 3, 1968: A GREAT DAY–"I WOULD LIKE TO LIVE"

Bishop Charles Mason Temple and the "I've Been to the Mountaintop" speech. For a complete audio of this speech, go to: http://

www.americanrhetoric.com/speeches/mlkivebeentothemountaintop
.htm and excerpted video at http://www.youtube.com/watch?v=Q
-OIjLDMWec For the complete text, go to: http://kingencyclopedia
.stanford.edu/encyclopedia/documentsentry/ive_been_to_the
_mountaintop/, and Carson, *A Call to Conscience*, 201–223.

APRIL 4, 1968: THE LAST DAY

King's and Ray's movements. As sourced above.

PART FOUR: MANHUNT!

ESCAPING MEMPHIS

The King assassination. The most comprehensive and authoritative books on the King murder are Sides, *Hellhound on His Trail*, and Posner, *Killing the Dream.*

Witness statements. All quotations are taken directly from the FBI Investigative Report: Shelby County Register of Deeds. *Dr. Martin Luther King, Jr. Assassination Investigation*, http://register.shelby.tn .us/media/mlk/index.php?album=FBI+Investigative+Repor

Police audio dispatches. All quotes are taken verbatim from the audio record. Audio File: http://register.shelby.tn.us/media/mlk /index.php?album=Audio+Files.

Ray's escape from Memphis. The most comprehensive treatment can be found in Sides, *Hellhound on His Trail*.

AFTERMATH AT THE MOTEL AND ACROSS THE NATION

LBJ's initial response. Sides's *Hellhound on His Trail* provides a detailed account of Johnson's activities.

The riots throughout the country. See Clay Risen, *A Nation on Fire: America in the Wake of the King Assassination* (Hoboken: John Wiley & Sons, 2009); and Ben W. Gilbert and the staff of the *Washington Post*, *Ten Blocks from the White House: Anatomy of the Washington Riots of 1968* (New York: F. A. Praeger, 1968).

RFK's Indianapolis address. The text of the entire speech can be found on the John F. Kennedy Presidential Library and Museum website at http://www.jfklibrary.org/Research/Research-Aids/Ready -Reference/RFK-Speeches/Statement-on-the-Assassination-of-Martin -Luther-King.aspx. For the complete audio and video, go to: https:// www.youtube.com/watch?v=GoKzCff8Zbs. See also Arthur M. Schlesinger, Jr., *Robert Kennedy and His Times* (Boston: Houghton Mifflin, 1978), 873–875.

Hoover's views on King and FBI activities. In addition to Garrow's *The FBI and Martin Luther King, Jr.*, see also Gerald McKnight, *The Last Crusade: Martin Luther King Jr., the FBI, and the Poor People's Campaign* (Boulder: Westview Press, 1998); Michael Friedly and

David Gallen, *Martin Luther King., Jr.: The FBI File* (New York: Carroll & Graf, 1993); and Kenneth O'Reilly, *Black Americans: The FBI Files* (New York: Carroll & Graf, 1994). See also U.S. Senate, *Supplemental Detailed Staff Reports on Intelligence Activities and the Rights of Americans,* Final Report of the Select Committee to Study Governmental Operations with Respect to Intelligence Activities, 94th Congress, 2nd Session, Senate Report 94–755 (Washington, DC: Government Printing Office, April 23, 1976), Book III ("the Church Committee"). (This volume specifically related to FBI, COIN-TELPRO, and Martin Luther King, Jr.). http://www.aarclibrary .org/publib/church/reports/book3/html/ChurchB3_0001a.htm. An examination of the FBI activities concerning the surveillance of King was published in January 1977, U.S. Department of Justice, *Report of the Department of Justice Task Force to Review the FBI Martin Luther King, Jr. Security and Assassination Investigation* (Washington, DC: The Task Force, 1977), https://vault.fbi.gov/Martin%20Luther %20King%2C%20Jr./Martin%20Luther%20King%2C%20Jr. %20Part%201%20of%202/view

FBI INVESTIGATION

The most comprehensive treatment of the FBI investigation can be found in the House Select Committee on Assassination's *Final Report* and appendixes volumes. A good summary appears in several chapters in the Sides book.

FAREWELL TO A KING

King's funeral. For the most complete account of the funeral of Martin Luther King, Jr., see Rebecca Burns, *Burial for a King: Martin Luther King Jr.'s Funeral and the Week That Transformed Atlanta and Rocked the Nation* (New York: Scribner, 2011). The funeral was widely reported by the mass market magazines at the time, with full-page front covers of first King and then his wife in grief, *Life* 64 and 65, no. 15 and 16 (April 12 and 19, 1968). One weekly magazine had a most graphic photograph of King in repose in an open casket with a mourner weeping, *Newsweek* 71, no. 16 (April 16, 1968); and the two major African American publications also had front-page stories: *JET* XXXXIV, no. 2 (April 18, 1968) and *Ebony* 23, no. 7 (May 1968).

The reinternment of King. South-View Cemetery was not Martin Luther King Jr.'s final resting place. A few years after his death, Coretta Scott King exhumed his remains. A new tomb/sarcophagus consisting of Georgia marble was placed in a lot cleared adjacent to the Ebenezer Baptist Church in Atlanta. This second gravesite and the "historic district" evolved over time. The Martin Luther King, Jr. Center for Nonviolent Social Change was built on this land with a plaza surrounded by arch-covered walkways. In time, a reflecting pool was added with the grave on a middle island of brick and concrete with a raised sarcophagus. In addition, across from the tomb, an eternal flame was installed. The third and final internment consisted of a larger sarcophagus when Coretta was laid to rest next to him in 2006, after her body was temporarily stored in a mausoleum at

South-View Cemetery. See https://www.nps.gov/malu/planyourvisit /the_king_center.htm and https://cemeterytravel.com/2012/01/11 /cemetery-of-the-week-46-the-martin-luther-king-jr-grave-site/

Souvenirs, magazine tributes. Similar to the aftermath of the JFK and RFK assassinations, many souvenir items were produced—even more so when the assassination of Robert Kennedy occurred a few months later.

Single-issue magazines flooded the newsstands in 1968, such as *Three Mothers, Their Life Stories: How Tragedy Made Them Sisters; Mrs. Robert Kennedy, Mrs. Martin Luther King, Jr., Mrs. John F. Kennedy* (New York: Macfadden-Bartell, 1968); *Memorial Martin Luther King,* Collectors Edition (New York: Country Wide Publications, 1968); *Martin Luther King, Jr., Journey of a Martyr* (New York: Award Books, 1968); *Martin Luther King, Jr., His Life, His Death* (Fort Worth, TX: SEPIA Publishing, 1968); *Martin Luther King, Jr.: His Dream Marches On* (New York: KMR Publications, 1968); and *United in Grief, Three Widows Share Their Sorrow: A Photographic Report of the Aftermath of Three Assassinations,* Collectors Edition (Washington, DC: Metro Publishers Representatives, 1968).

Phonograph records. Several long-play 33-1/3 RPM tribute, memorial, and funeral phonographic records were also released, such as *Dr. Martin Luther King, Jr.: Funeral Services Ebenezer Baptist Church, April 9, 1968—Plus Last Great Speeches,* Brotherhood

Records, 1969 (LP Stereo 2001); *Free at Last: Dr. Martin Luther King, Jr.,* Gordy Records, 1968 (929); *I Have a Dream: The Rev. Dr. Martin Luther King, Jr., 1929–1968,* 20th Century Fox, 1968 (TFS-3201 Stereo); and *The Rev. Dr. Martin Luther King, Jr.: In Search of Freedom,* Mercury Records, 1968 (SR-61170). Scores of additional tributes, memorials, and famous speeches would be issued in the decades to follow.

Hand fans. Many variant church and funeral chapel cardboard hand fans were mass produced with the pictures of the three martyrs—RFK, JFK, and King—on the front side ("These Americans died for Freedom"), or King and his mother after her death ("Together Again") and/or his parents, or King by himself. On the back side appeared the name of the individual church or funeral parlor.

Pin-back buttons and pennants. A few were immediately made after King's death, such as the WE MOURN OUR LOSS and the I HAVE A DREAM; LET FREEDOM RING pin-backs. And over the years, hundreds of commemorative buttons have been manufactured to celebrate various anniversaries.

Tapestries. Also, especially after the assassination of RFK, tapestries were produced with images of JFK, RFK, and King.

APRIL 16-20, 1968: THE ASSASSIN IDENTIFIED

Frank, Huie, Posner, and Sides are the best sources.

JUNE 4-8, 1968: ANOTHER ASSASSINATION AND AN ARREST

The assassination of Robert F. Kennedy. Many works were published on the death of Robert F. Kennedy, but perhaps the best place to start is Robert Blair Kaiser, *"R.F.K. Must Die!": A History of the Robert Kennedy Assassination and Its Aftermath* (New York: E. P. Dutton, 1970); and Robert A. Houghton and Theodore Taylor, *Special Unit Senator: The Investigation of the Assassination of Senator Robert F. Kennedy* (New York: Random House, 1970).

ABC TV series *The F.B.I.* The identification of James Earl Ray on the FBI's Most Wanted list occurred at the end of Season 3, Episode 26, "The Tunnel," on April 21, 1968, in which the FBI pursues bank robbers who successfully dig a tunnel to break into a bank vault.

Ray's movements after the assassination. The most important record of Ray's movements and his comments about his eluding capture can be found in the multivolume House Select Committee on Assassination. U.S. House of Representatives, *Select Committee on Assassinations* (13 volumes), "The Investigation of the Assassination of Martin Luther King," and the one-volume "Final Report," 95th Congress, 2nd Session (Washington, DC: Government Printing Office, 1979): https://www.fbi.gov/wantedhttps://www.fbi.gov/wanted (The narrative of Ray's escape can be found in Volume III.) The volumes are available online at http://www.maryferrell.org/php/showlist.php?docset=1573. This site also contains additional FBI files, including the FBI's MURKIN documents.

Ray's extradition to the United States. See *The James Earl Ray Extradition File: Papers Submitted to Great Britain for the Extradition of James Earl Ray to Face Trial for the Murder of Martin Luther King, Jr.* (New York: Lemma Publishing, 1971). To see a short video of Ray being read his rights by U.S. authorities and then being searched and examined by Shelby County authorities, go to: https://www .youtube.com/watch?v=cWB6dNsNaAU

Ray's guilty plea. One of Ray's early lawyers, prominent Texas attorney Percy Foreman, initially convinced him to plead guilty to avoid the death penalty. Shortly after the plea was entered and sentencing was imposed, Ray fired Foreman and began his odyssey of attempting legal steps for withdrawing the guilty plea. Over the years of his incarceration, Ray continued to seek a new trial, represented by several different attorneys. The first of at least seven attempts for post-conviction relief in both state and federal court can be found at *Ray v. State*, 224 Tenn 164, 461 S.W. 2nd 854 (Tenn. 1970), and the last at *Ray v. State*, 984 S.W. 2nd 239 (Tenn. App. 1998). Some of the cases in between these dates ended up with the United States Supreme Court denying review. Ray was quite litigious, bringing defamation cases against individuals when he was in prison. Also, his brother Jerry pursued legal action to obtain some of Ray's property held by the State of Tennessee, which was to be used in the prosecution of Ray (left behind at the Memphis rooming house after he shot King).

Almost immediately after the guilty plea, as Ray claimed his innocence, he began his "story" about the mysterious Raoul as the person behind the assassination. In fact, one of the early biographers of Ray, journalist William Bradford Huie, began to write a book and a series of *Look* magazine articles but soon doubted Ray's claims in his "20,000 words" account. The title of Huie's book was changed from *They Slew the Dreamer* to *He Slew the Dreamer.* Years later, the book was published in trade paperback with the enticing title *Did the FBI Kill Martin Luther King?* His conclusion in the new preface was the same—James Earl Ray acted alone.

Conspiracy theories. When James Earl Ray first pled guilty, there was no trial. Subsequently, he professed his innocence with many, sometimes inconsistent and contrary statements in his own authored books, his interviews in national magazines, and his testimony before and interviews to the U.S. House of Representatives Select Committee on Assassinations (HSCA). So the fertile soil for conspiracy theories had been laid down. To complicate matters, FBI surveillance and government misconduct concerning King added to the suspicions that the federal government had something more to conceal, or was actually involved in the assassination.

And long before the "Son of Sam" laws, which prohibit convicted criminals from financially benefiting by authoring or cowriting a book on their crimes, Huie, a bestselling journalist, saw a money-making opportunity. To gain access to Ray, he entered into a book-and-magazine contract, where representations were made to share in the profits to pay for the legal defense—and some money going to Ray himself.

The most prominent of all conspiracy theorists, attorney Mark Lane, made his appearance on the subject in the 1970s. He joined with Dick Gregory to cowrite the book *Code Name "Zorro": The Murder of Martin Luther King, Jr.* (Englewood Cliffs: Prentice-Hall, 1977). Lane also represented James Earl Ray before the HSCA.

Jim Garrison, the district attorney who unsuccessfully prosecuted New Orleans businessman Clay Shaw in 1967 for conspiring to kill JFK, frequently announced to the public that the same diabolical force was behind the murders of John Kennedy, Robert Kennedy, and Martin Luther King, Jr.

Other first-generation JFK conspiracy "buffs" also joined in the chorus of questioning Ray's guilt and whether he acted alone, including Harold Weisberg in *Frame-Up: The Martin Luther King/James Earl Ray Case Containing Suppressed Evidence* (New York: Outerbridge & Dienstfrey, 1971). Not surprisingly, some King conspiracy proponents wrote books about President Kennedy's assassination as well. And new generations of JFK assassination-conspiracy writers continue to author books on the King murder.

By the mid-1970s, the clamoring of notions of conspiracy and government cover-ups led to the formation of a House of Representatives Select Committee on Assassinations (HSCA) to investigate the murders of President John F. Kennedy and Dr. Martin Luther King, Jr. Typical of congressional investigations, the findings usually reflect public sentiment. The findings of a "second" gunman in the JFK assassination relied on later-discredited acoustics evidence, and for King, there was an equally unsupported proposition.

James Earl Ray, as the master con man, liar, and criminal, perhaps recognized the penchant of this conspiracy community to accept wild stories of government cover-up. Ray claimed his innocence and invented the mysterious Raoul, who allegedly told him what to do regarding the King assassination. The HSCA thoroughly investigated these conspiracy motifs and found no credibility to them whatsoever. See U.S. House of Representatives, *Select Committee on Assassinations*, "The Investigation of the Assassination of Martin Luther King; Final Report," 95th Congress, 2nd Session (Washington, DC: Government Printing Office, 1979). The Report of the HSCA is also at http://www .archives.gov/research/jfk/select-committee-report/part-2c.html

The committee concluded that Ray alone shot King. Nevertheless, the chairman of the committee, Congressman Louis Stokes (D-OH), ultimately bowed to public opinion, stating in the final report that the Department of Justice and the FBI "failed to investigate adequately the possibility of conspiracy in the assassination." There was no evidence to back up the statement. See HSCA "Final Report," pp. 5–6, at http://history-matters.com/archive/contents/hsca/contents_hsca _report.htm. Stokes also stated that "The Committee Believes that Based on Circumstantial Evidence Available to It, that there is a likelihood that James Earl Ray Assassinated Dr. Martin Luther King Jr., as a Result of a Conspiracy." See HSCA "Final Report," pp. 325–374. In addition, there was definitive proof of misconduct in the surveillance of King. These conclusions were an invitation for the conspiracy theorists community to continue to search for the "truth."

Over the years, books and articles were written, including those authored by Ray's brothers, tying the assassination of King to a myriad of groups such as the Ku Klux Klan, various white supremacists, the FBI, and the CIA. Some claimed links to organized crime boss Carlos Marcello and Ray's trip to New Orleans. Others place the mysterious Raoul as one of the "tramps" in Dealey Plaza who were rounded up by the police and never identified—a part of numerous conspiracy theories on the JFK assassination. Contradictory and competing theories abound on the King assassination.

This all culminated with attorney William Pepper writing three books on the King assassination. See William F. Pepper, *Orders to Kill: The Truth Behind the Murder of Martin Luther King, Jr.* (New York: Warner Books, 1998); *An Act of State: The Execution of Martin Luther King* (New York: Verso, 2008); and the revised version updated and expanded as *The Plot to Kill King: The Truth behind the Assassination of Martin Luther King, Jr.* (New York: Skyhorse Publishing, 2016). Pepper, as yet another attorney representing Ray, convinced a still-grieving King family that the civil rights leader had indeed been killed by diabolical forces and Ray was innocent. Pepper represented Coretta Scott King and her family in the Tennessee wrongful death civil suit against Loyd Jowers, the owner of a restaurant near the Lorraine Motel, alleging a mafia and U.S. government conspiracy to kill King. Jowers claimed that he hired a Memphis police officer who fired the fatal shot—and that James Earl Ray was innocent. The jurors accepted this version—although much contradictory evidence was admitted, and a good deal of the evidence against Ray was omitted from the trial. It would not be the first time that the civil justice system had failed in discovering the truth. In 2000, the Department of Justice had no choice but to issue yet one more report, totally refuting this civil verdict. For the complete transcript of the civil trial, see http://www.thekingcenter.org/civil-case-king-family-versus-jowers, and for the U.S. Department of Justice's response, see https://www.justice.gov/crt/united-states-department-justice-investigation-recent-allegations-regarding-assassination-dr and https://www.justice.gov/crt/list-attachments-0

In the final analysis, one is left with the distinct possibility that the only conspiracy may have been that one or both of Ray's brothers supported him financially, sending him money before or after the assassination while he was eluding the FBI. But that is about it. Also, the most convincing witness that Ray acted alone is James Earl Ray himself—confirmed by his contradictory statements and his testimony to the HSCA (his oral testimony before the committee, Volume II of the HSCA Report; his eight long interviews by the HSCA in the Appendix volumes IX through XI; his essay of "20,000 words" in Volume XII; the Compilation of His Statements in Volume III of the Report; his two books and countless interviews). Ray proved to everyone that he was not a credible witness. After its extensive investigation, the HSCA concluded that Raoul did not exist and that "Ray's post-assassination tale of Raoul was fabricated." (HSCA, "Final Report," 303–306).

A YEAR LIKE NO OTHER

Dion's "Abraham, Martin and John." This song was written by Dick Holler. It was first performed by Dion (Dion Francis DeMucci) and released on Laurie Records as a 45 RPM single in August 1968. Listen at https://www.youtube.com/watch?v=rDOmf5ER0-M. The sheet music was originally published in 1968 by Roznique Music of New York City, with images of JFK; RFK; Martin Luther King, Jr.; and Abraham Lincoln superimposed on Mount Rushmore. See http://www.lincolncollection.org/collection/creator-author/item/?cs =R&creator=Roznique+Music%2C+Inc.&item=22866

In the months and years that followed, many other well-known African American performers released their own 45 RPM singles of this song, including Smokey Robinson and the Miracles, Harry Belafonte, Moms Mabley, Mahalia Jackson, and Marvin Gaye. Also, in 1971, the song was featured in Tom Clay's "What the World Needs Now Is Love/ Abraham, Martin and John." This medley combined Dion's recording with Jackie DeShannon's version of Burt Bacharach's "What the World Needs Now," and with vocals by the Blackberries. In addition, Clay's recording features a narration in which an adult asked a child to define several words associated with racism, such as *segregation*. Also, there were sound bites of speeches, a radio re-creation of the JFK assassination, voices from the Ambassador Hotel kitchen after RFK had been shot, and Edward Kennedy's eulogy for yet another one of his brothers who was killed. For the original recording, go to: https://www .youtube.com/watch?v=uEyFxPD8KBc. For a recent version of this Clay interpretation, bringing it up-to-date by including some of

President Obama's remarks, go to: https://www.youtube.com/watch?v =MWW24zbHM2U

Apollo 8 Christmas message. Go to: http://www.nasa.gov/topics /history/features/apollo_8.html. Also go to: https://www.nasa.gov /mission_pages/apollo/missions/apollo8.html#.V0EmN9QrJgt

EPILOGUE

Martin Luther King, Jr. National Historic Site. See the National Park Service webpage: https://www.nps.gov/mlkm/index.htm

LBJ's last public address. The December 12, 1972, address was given at the LBJ Presidential Library just a few months before his death. For a video of the complete remarks, go to: http://www .c-span.org/video/?320205-1/lyndon-johnson-civil-rights

Hoover's death. See the obituary in the *New York Times*, May 3, 1972, at http://www.nytimes.com/learning/general/onthisday/bday /0101.html

King's mother's death. See front-page story by B. Drummond Ayers, Jr., "Mother of Dr. King Is Killed in Church; Atlanta Deacon Slain; Gunman Seized: Police Doubt Black Youth Was Part of Conspiracy," and numerous additional stories in the *New York Times*, July 1, 1974.

Ray's escape from prison. See front-page story "James Earl Ray Flees a Prison in Tennessee with 6 Other Convicts; Convicted Slayer of Dr. King Uses Ladder of Wire to Scale Wall," *New York Times,* June 11, 1977, and the *Time* magazine cover story "The Escape," *Time,* LXXIX, no. 25 (June 20, 1977).

Dexter King's meeting with Ray in prison. See the MSNBC clip at https://www.youtube.com/watch?v=-wHQZ1zyVxY Also see Kevin Sachs, "Dr. King's Son Says Family Believes Ray Is Innocent," *New York Times,* March 28, 1997, http://www.nytimes.com/1997/03/28 /us/dr-king-s-son-says-family-believes-ray-is-innocent.html

Abernathy's death. See the obituary in the *New York Times,* April 18, 1990, http://www.nytimes.com/learning/general/onthisday/bday /0311.html

Coretta Scott King's death. See the obituary in the *New York Times,* February 1, 2006, http://www.nytimes.com/2006/02/01/national /01king.html?pagewanted=all

For her autobiography, see Coretta Scott King, *My Life with Martin Luther King, Jr.* (New York: Holt, Rinehart and Winston, 1969), and also Coretta Scott King and Rev. Dr. Barbara Reynolds, *My Life, My Love, My Legacy* (New York: Henry Holt and Company, 2017).

Izola Curry's death. See the obituary in the *New York Times,* March 21, 2015, http://www.nytimes.com/2015/03/22/us/izola-ware-curry -who-stabbed-king-in-1958-dies-at-98.html?_r=0

The old magazines and newspapers from the 1950s and 1960s are wonderful time capsules that give a sense of what it was like to be living in America during the era of Martin Luther King, Jr. *Life* and *Look*, the big weekly illustrated news magazines, gave extensive coverage to the assassination of Dr. King and the manhunt for James Earl Ray, as did African American magazines like *JET* and *Ebony*. The major city newspapers in Atlanta; Birmingham; Memphis; Richmond; Chicago; Los Angeles; Dallas; Washington, DC; and New York City covered Martin Luther King, Jr., extensively, as did the African American newspapers like the *Chicago Defender* or *New York Amsterdam News*. Ask your librarian to help you find old newspaper stories on microfilm or the Internet.

WORKS BY KING

A Comparison of the Conceptions of God and the Thinking of Paul Tillich and Henry Nelson Wieman. Boston University, 1955. (Doctoral dissertation)

Letter from Birmingham Jail. American Friends Service Committee, 1963.

The Measure of a Man. Philadelphia: Christian Education Press, 1959.

The Papers of Martin Luther King, Jr. Volume I: Called to Serve, January 1929–June 1951. Berkeley: University of California Press, 1992.

The Papers of Martin Luther King, Jr. Volume II: Rediscovering Precious Values, July 1951–November 1955. Berkeley: University of California Press, 1994.

The Papers of Martin Luther King, Jr. Volume III: Birth of a New Age, December 1955–December 1956. Berkeley: University of California Press, 1997.

The Papers of Martin Luther King, Jr. Volume IV: Symbol of the Movement, January 1957–December 1958. Berkeley: University of California Press, 2000.

The Papers of Martin Luther King, Jr. Volume V: Threshold of a New Decade, January 1959–December 1960. Berkeley: University of California Press, 2005.

The Papers of Martin Luther King, Jr. Volume VI: Advocate of the Social Gospel, September 1948–March 1963. Berkeley: University of California Press, 2007.

The Papers of Martin Luther King, Jr. Volume VII: To Save the Soul of America, January 1961–August 1962. Berkeley: University of California Press, 2014.

Strength to Love. New York: Harper & Row, 1963. (collection of sermons).

Stride Toward Freedom: A Leader of His People Tells the Montgomery Story. New York: Harper & Row, 1958.

The Trumpet of Conscience. New York: Harper & Row, 1968. (collection of lectures).

Where Do We Go from Here: Chaos or Community? New York: Harper & Row, 1967.

Why We Can't Wait. New York: Harper & Row, 1964.

ALSO, THESE EDITED WORKS:

Carson, Clayborne, and Kris Shepard, eds. *A Call to Conscience: The Landmark Speeches of Dr. Martin Luther King.* New York: Warner Books, 2001.

Carson, Clayborne, and Peter Holloran, eds. *A Knock at Midnight: Inspiration from the Great Sermons of Reverend Martin Luther King, Jr.* New York: Warner Books, 1998.

Garrow, David J., ed. *Martin Luther King, Jr.: Civil Rights Leader, Theologian, Orator.* In 3 volumes. Brooklyn: Carlson Publishing, 1989.

Washington, James Melvin, ed. *A Testament of Hope: The Essential Writings of Dr. Martin Luther King, Jr.* San Francisco: Harper & Row, 1986.

Many of King's speeches, sermons, letters, etc., are available online at the Martin Luther King, Jr. Research and Education Institute at Stanford University: https://kinginstitute.stanford.edu/

WORKS ABOUT KING BY FAMILY MEMBERS

Carson, Clayborne, ed. *The Autobiography of Martin Luther King, Jr.* New York: Warner Books, 1998.

Farris, Christine King. *Through It All: Reflections on My Life, My Family, and My Faith.* New York: Atria Books, 2009.

King, Coretta Scott. *My Life with Martin Luther King, Jr.* New York: Holt, Rinehart and Winston, 1969.

King, Coretta Scott, as told to Rev. Dr. Barbara Reynolds. *My Life, My Love, My Legacy*. New York: Henry Holt and Company, 2017.

King, Dexter Scott, and Ralph Wiley. *Growing Up King: An Intimate Memoir*. New York: IPM, 2003.

King, Martin Luther, Sr., and Clayton Riley. *Daddy King: An Autobiography*. New York: William Morrow, 1980.

Watkins, Angela Farris, and Andrew Young, eds. *Martin Luther King, Jr.: A Family Tribute*. New York: Abrams, 2012.

CHILDREN'S BOOKS ABOUT KING BY FAMILY MEMBERS

Farris, Christine King. *March On!: The Day My Brother Martin Changed the World*. New York: Scholastic Press, 2008.

———. *Martin Luther King, Jr.: His Life and Dream*. Lexington: Silver Burdett Ginn, 1986.

———. *My Brother Martin: A Sister Remembers Growing Up with Rev. Dr. Martin Luther King, Jr.* New York: Simon & Schuster, 2003.

Watkins, Angela Farris. *My Uncle Martin's Big Heart*. New York: Abrams Books for Young Readers, 2010.

——. *My Uncle Martin's Words for America: Martin Luther King Jr.'s Niece Tells How He Made a Difference*. New York: Abrams Books for Young Readers, 2011.

WORKS ABOUT KING (GENERAL)

Bagley, Edythe Scott, with Joe Hilley. *Desert Rose: The Life and Legacy of Coretta Scott King*. Tuscaloosa: University of Alabama Press, 2012.

Bennett, Lerone, Jr. *What Manner of Man: A Biography of Martin Luther King, Jr., 1929–1968*. Chicago: Johnson Publishing, 1964. 4th revised edition, 1976.

Bishop, Jim. *In the Days of Martin Luther King, Jr.* New York: G. P. Putnam's Sons, 1971.

Burns, Stewart. *To the Mountaintop: Martin Luther King, Jr.'s Mission to Save America: 1955–1968*. New York: HarperSanFrancisco, 2004.

Cone, James H. *Martin & Malcolm & America: A Dream or a Nightmare*. Maryknoll: Orbis Books, 1991.

Dyson, Michael Eric. *I May Not Get There with You: The True Martin Luther King, Jr.* New York: Free Press, 2000.

Fairclough, Adam. *Martin Luther King, Jr.* Athens: University of Georgia Press, 1995.

Frady, Marshall. *Martin Luther King, Jr.: A Life.* New York: Penguin Group, 2002.

Garrow, David J. *Bearing the Cross: Martin Luther King, Jr., and the Southern Christian Leadership Conference.* New York: William Morrow, 1986.

Jackson, Thomas F. *From Civil Rights to Human Rights: Martin Luther King, Jr., and the Struggle for Economic Justice.* Philadelphia: University of Pennsylvania Press, 2007.

Jackson, Troy. *Becoming King: Martin Luther King Jr. and the Making of a National Leader.* Lexington: University of Kentucky Press, 2008.

Johnson, Charles, and Bob Adelman. *King: A Photobiography of Martin Luther King, Jr.* New York: Viking Studio, 2000.

King: A Filmed Record . . . From Montgomery to Memphis. 1970 documentary film converted to DVD by Kino Lorber Films, 2013. 185 minutes. (2 DVDs)

Lentz, Richard. *Symbols, the News Magazines, and Martin Luther King.* Baton Rouge: Louisiana State University Press, 1990.

Lewis, David L. *King: A Critical Biography.* New York: Praeger, 1970. Expanded 3rd edition, Urbana: University of Illinois Press, 2013.

Life magazine, eds. *Remembering Dr. Martin Luther King: His Life and Crusade in Pictures.* New York: *Life* Magazine, 2008.

Lincoln, C. Eric, ed. *Martin Luther King, Jr.: A Profile.* New York: Hill and Wang, 1970.

Lischer, Richard. *The Preacher King: Martin Luther King, Jr. and the Word That Moved America.* New York: Oxford University Press, 1995.

Martin Luther King, Jr., and the Global Freedom Struggle, Encyclopedia (online): http://mlk-kpp01.stanford.edu/index.php /encyclopedia/encyclopedia_contents

Miller, Keith. *Voice of Deliverance: The Language of Martin Luther King, Jr., and Its Sources.* New York: The Free Press, 1992.

Miller, William. *Martin Luther King Jr.: His Life, Martyrdom, and Meaning for the World.* New York: Weybright and Talley, 1968.

Oates, Stephen. *Let the Trumpet Sound: The Life of Martin Luther King, Jr.* New York: Harper & Row, 1982.

Pearson, Hugh. *When Harlem Nearly Killed King: The 1958 Stabbing of Dr. Martin Luther King, Jr.* New York: Seven Stories Press, 2002.

Reddick, Lawrence D. *Crusader without Violence: A Biography of Martin Luther King, Jr.* New York: Harper and Brothers, 1959.

Reider, Jonathan. *The Word of the Lord Is Upon Me: The Righteous Performance of Martin Luther King, Jr.* Cambridge, MA: The Belknap Press of Harvard University Press, 2008.

Sunnemark, Fredrik. *Ring Out Freedom!: The Voice of Martin Luther King, Jr. and the Making of the Civil Rights Movement.* Bloomington: Indiana University Press, 2004.

Witherspoon, William Roger. *Martin Luther King, Jr.: To the Mountaintop.* Garden City: Doubleday, 1985.

KING BIBLIOGRAPHIES

Fisher, William H., comp. *Free at Last: A Bibliography of Martin Luther King, Jr.* Metuchen: Scarecrow Press, 1977.

Pyatt, Sherman E., comp. *Martin Luther King, Jr.: An Annotated Bibliography.* New York: Greenwood Press, 1986.

MAJOR KING INSTITUTIONS ONLINE

The Martin Luther King, Jr. Center for Nonviolent Social Change, Atlanta, Georgia: http://www.thekingcenter.org/

The Martin Luther King, Jr. Research and Education Institute, Stanford University: https://kinginstitute.stanford.edu/. This site includes the King Papers Project: https://kinginstitute.stanford.edu /king-papers/about-papers-project

Martin Luther King, Jr. National Historical Site, Atlanta, Georgia (birth home, Ebenezer Baptist Church, and the gravesite at the King Center): http://www.nps.gov/malu/index.htm

National Civil Rights Museum, at the Lorraine Motel, Memphis, Tennessee: http://www.civilrightsmuseum.org/

CIVIL RIGHTS MOVEMENT AND MARTIN LUTHER KING, JR. (INDIVIDUAL FIRSTHAND ACCOUNTS BY CIVIL RIGHTS ACTIVISTS)

Abernathy, Ralph David. *And the Walls Came Tumbling Down: An Autobiography*. New York: Harper & Row, 1989.

Albert, Peter J. and Ronald Hoffman, eds. *We Shall Overcome: Martin Luther King, Jr. and the Black Freedom Struggle*. New York: Pantheon Books (in cooperation with the United States Capitol Historical Society), 1990.

Baldwin, James. *The Fire Next Time*. New York: Dial Press, 1963.

————. *No Name in the Street*. New York: Dial Press, 1972.

Bates, Daisy. *The Long Shadow of Little Rock: A Memoir*. New York: David MacKay Company, 1962.

Beals, Melba Pattillo. *Warriors Don't Cry: A Searing Memoir of the Battle to Integrate Little Rock's Central High*. New York: Washington Square Press, 1994.

Beifuss, Joan Turner. *At the River I Stand: Memphis, the 1968 Strike, and Martin Luther King.* Brooklyn: Carlson Publishing, 1989.

Burns, Stewart, ed. *Daybreak of Freedom: The Montgomery Bus Boycott.* Chapel Hill: University of North Carolina Press, 1997.

Carson, Clayborne. *Martin's Dream: My Journey and the Legacy of Martin Luther King Jr.* New York: Palgrave Macmillan, 2013.

————. *In Struggle: SNCC and the Black Awakening of the 1960s.* Cambridge: Harvard University Press, 1981.

Carson, Clayborne; David J. Garrow; Gerald Gill; Vincent Harding; and Darlene Clark Hine, eds. *The Eyes on the Prize Civil Rights Reader: Documents, Speeches, and Firsthand Accounts from the Black Freedom Struggle.* New York: Viking Penguin, 1991.

Chestnut, J. L., Jr. and Julia Cass. *Black in Selma: The Uncommon Life of J. L. Chestnut, Jr.* New York: Farrar, Straus, and Giroux, 1990.

Clayton, Xernova. *I've Been Marching All the Time: An Autobiography.* Athens: Longstreet Press, 1991.

Crawford, Vicki L., Jacqueline Anne Rouse, and Barbara Woods, eds. *Women in the Civil Rights Movement: Trailblazers and Torchbearers, 1941–1965.* Brooklyn: Carlson, 1990.

Evers, Mrs. Medgar (Myrlie Evers-Williams), with William Peters. *For Us, the Living.* Garden City: Doubleday, 1967.

Farmer, James. *Lay Bare My Heart: An Autobiography of the Civil Rights Movement.* New York: Arbor House, 1985.

Fields, Uriah J. *Inside the Montgomery Bus Boycott: My Personal Story.* Baltimore: America House, 2002.

Forman, James. *The Making of Black Revolutionaries: A Personal Account.* New York: Macmillan, 1972.

Gilliard, Deric A. *Living in the Shadow of a Legend: Unsung Heroes and "Sheroes" Who Marched with Martin Luther King, Jr.* Decatur: Gilliard Communications, 2002.

Gray, Fred D. *Bus Ride to Freedom: The Life and Works of Fred Gray.* Montgomery: Black Belt Press, 1995.

Hampton, Henry, Steve Faver, and Sarah Flynn, comps. *Voices of Freedom: An Oral History of the Civil Rights Movement from the 1950s through the 1980s.* New York: Bantam Books, 1990.

Hansberry, Lorraine. *The Movement: Documentary of a Struggle for Equality.* New York: Simon and Schuster, 1964.

Harding, Vincent. *Hope and History: Why We Must Share the History of the Movement*. Maryknoll: Orbis Books, 1990.

Hedgeman, Anna Arnold. *The Trumpet Sounds: A Memoir of Negro Leadership*. New York: Holt, Rinehart and Winston, 1964.

Holsaert, Faith S.; Martha Prescod; Norman Noonan; Judy Richardson; Betty Garman Robinson; Jean Smith Young; and Dorothy M. Zellner, eds. *Hands on the Freedom Plow: Personal Accounts by the Women in SNCC*. Champaign-Urbana: University of Illinois Press, 2010.

Holt, Len. *The Summer That Didn't End*. New York: William Morrow, 1965.

Hughes, Langston. *Fight for Freedom: The Story of the NAACP*. New York: W. W. Norton & Co., 1962.

Jackson, Jesse, and Elaine Landau. *Black in America: A Fight for Freedom*. New York: J. Messer, 1973.

Jones, Clarence, and Stuart Connelly. *Behind the Dream: The Making of a Speech That Transformed a Nation*. New York: Palgrave Macmillan, 2011.

King, Mary. Freedom Song: *A Personal Story of the 1960s Civil Rights Movement*. New York: William Morrow, 1987.

Levine, Ellen, ed. *Freedom's Children: Young Civil Rights Activists Tell Their Own Stories.* New York: G. P. Putnam's Sons, 1993.

Lewis, John, and Andrew Aydin. *March.* (Books One, Two, and Three). Marietta: Top Shelf Productions, 2013, 2015, 2016.

Lewis, John, and Michael D'Orso. *Walking with the Wind: A Memoir of the Movement.* New York: Simon & Schuster, 1998.

Mays, Benjamin. *Born to Rebel: An Autobiography.* New York: Scribner, 1971.

McKissick, Floyd B. *Three-Fifths of a Man.* New York: Macmillan, 1969.

Meredith, James. *A Mission from God: A Memoir and Challenge for America.* New York: Atria Books, 2012.

Meredith, James, and William Doyle. *Three Years in Mississippi.* Bloomington: Indiana University Press, 1966.

Moody, Anne. *Coming of Age in Mississippi: The Classic Autobiography of Growing Up Poor and Black in the Rural South.* New York: Dial Press, 1968.

Parks, Rosa, and Jim Haskins. *Rosa Parks: My Story.* New York: Dial Books, 1992.

Powers, Georgia Davis. *I Shared the Dream: The Pride, Passion and Politics of the First Black Woman Senator from Kentucky*. Far Hills: New Horizon Press, 1995.

Raines, Howell, ed. *My Soul Is Rested: Movement Days in the Deep South Remembered*. New York: Penguin Books, 1983. Reprint edition of *My Soul Is Rested: The Story of the Civil Rights Movement in the Deep South*. New York: G. P. Putnam's Sons, 1977.

Robinson, Jo Ann Gibson. *The Montgomery Bus Boycott and the Women Who Started It: The Memoir of Jo Ann Gibson Robinson*. Edited by David J. Garrow. Knoxville: University of Tennessee Press, 1987.

Rustin, Bayard. *Down the Line: The Collected Writings of Bayard Rustin*. Chicago: Quadrangle Books, 1971.

Saunders, Doris E., ed. *The Day They Marched*. Chicago: Johnson Publishing Company, 1963.

Schulke, Flip. *He Had a Dream: Martin Luther King, Jr., and the Civil Rights Movement*. New York: W. W. Norton & Company, 1995.

Schulke, Flip, and Penelope Ortner McPhee. *King Remembered: The Story of Dr. Martin Luther King Jr. in Words and Pictures*. New York: W. W. Norton & Company, 1986.

Sellers, Cleveland, and Robert Terrell. *The River of No Return: The Autobiography of a Black Militant and the Life and Death of SNCC.* Jackson: University Press of Mississippi, 1990.

Webb, Sheyann, and Rachel West Nelson (as told to Frank Sikora). *Selma, Lord, Selma: Girlhood Memories of the Civil-Rights Days.* Birmingham: University of Alabama Press, 1980.

Wexler, Sanford, ed. *An Eyewitness History of the Civil Rights Movement.* New York: Facts on File, 1993.

Wilkins, Roy, and Tom Mathews. *Standing Fast: The Autobiography of Roy Wilkins.* New York: Da Capo Press, 1994.

Young, Andrew. *An Easy Burden: The Civil Rights Movement and the Transformation of America.* New York: HarperCollins Publishers, 1996.

Young Jr., Whitney M. *To Be Equal.* New York: McGraw-Hill, 1965.

CIVIL RIGHTS MOVEMENT (GENERAL)

Abernathy, Donzaleigh. *Partners to History: Martin Luther King Jr., Ralph David Abernathy, and the Civil Rights Movement.* New York: Crown Publishers, 2003.

Anderson, Jervis. *A. Philip Randolph: A Biographical Portrait.* New York: Harcourt Brace Jovanovich, 1973.

————. *Bayard Rustin: Troubles I've Seen: A Biography.* New York: HarperCollins Publishers, 1997.

Arsenault, Raymond. *Freedom Riders: 1961 and the Struggle for Racial Justice.* New York: Oxford University Press, 2006.

Bass, S. Jonathan. *Blessed Are the Peacemakers: Martin Luther King Jr., Eight White Religious Leaders, and the "Letter from Birmingham Jail."* Baton Rouge: Louisiana State University Press, 2001.

Berger, Maurice. *For All the World to See: Visual Culture and the Struggle for Civil Rights.* New Haven: Yale University Press, 2010.

Blake, John. *Children of the Movement: The Sons and Daughters of Martin Luther King Jr., Malcolm X, Elijah Muhammad, George*

Wallace, Andrew Young, Julian Bond, Stokely Carmichael, Bob Moses, James Chaney, Elaine Brown, and Others Reveal How the Civil Rights Movement Tested and Transformed Their Families. Chicago: Lawrence Hill Books, 2004.

Branch, Taylor. *At Canaan's Edge: America in the King Years, 1965–1968.* New York: Simon & Schuster, 2006.

———. *Parting the Waters: America in the King Years, 1954–1963.* New York: Simon & Schuster, 1989.

———. *Pillar of Fire: America in the King Years, 1963–1965.* New York: Simon & Schuster, 1998.

———. *The King Years: Historic Moments in the Civil Rights Movement.* New York: Simon & Schuster, 2013. (abridged version of the trilogy)

Burner, Eric. *And Gently He Shall Lead Them: Robert Parris Moses and Civil Rights in Mississippi.* New York: New York University Press, 1994.

Dickerson, Dennis C. *Militant Mediator: Whitney M. Young, Jr.* Lexington: University of Kentucky Press, 2004.

Dittmer, John. *Local People: The Struggle for Civil Rights in Mississippi.* Urbana: University of Illinois Press, 1994.

Dorman, Michael. *We Shall Overcome: A Reporter's Eyewitness Account of the Year of Racial Strife and Triumph.* New York: Delacorte Press, 1964.

Eagles, Charles W., ed. *The Civil Rights Movement in America.* Jackson: University Press of Mississippi, 1986.

Else, Jon. *True South: Henry Hampton and Eyes on the Prize, the Landmark Television Series That Reframed the Civil Rights Movement.* New York: Viking, 2017. Book to accompany PBS Video, Eyes on the Prize: America's Civil Rights Movement, Blackside, Inc., 2006. (Seven volume DVD series).

Eskew, Glenn T. *But for Birmingham: The Local and National Movements in the Civil Rights Struggle.* Chapel Hill: University of North Carolina Press, 1997.

Fairclough, Adam. *To Redeem the Soul of America: The Southern Christian Leadership Conference & Martin Luther King, Jr.* Athens: University of Georgia, 1987.

Garrow, David J., ed. *We Shall Overcome: The Civil Rights Movement in the United States in the 1950s and 1960s.* 3 volumes. Brooklyn: Carlson Publishing, 1989.

Grant, Joanne. *Ella Baker: Freedom Bound.* New York: Wiley, 1998.

Halberstam, David. *The Children*. New York: Random House, 1998.

Hogan, Wesley C. *Many Minds, One Heart: SNCC's Dream for a New America*. Chapel Hill: University of North Carolina Press, 2007.

Kasher, Steven. *The Civil Rights Movement: A Photographic History, 1954–68*. New York: Abbeville, Press, 1996.

Kirk, John A. *Martin Luther King, Jr. and the Civil Rights Movement: Controversies and Debates*. New York: Palgrave Macmillan, 2007.

Levy, Peter B. *The Civil Rights Movement*. Westport: Greenwood Press, 1998.

Manis, Andrew M. *A Fire You Can't Put Out: The Civil Rights Life of Birmingham's Reverend Fred Shuttlesworth*. Tuscaloosa: University of Alabama Press, 1999.

McAdam, Doug. *Freedom Summer*. New York: Oxford University Press, 1988.

McWhorter, Diane. *Carry Me Home: Birmingham, Alabama: The Climactic Battle of the Civil Rights Revolution*. New York: Simon & Schuster, 2001.

Marable, Manning. *Race, Reform, and Rebellion: The Second Recon-struction in Black American, 1943–1982.* Jackson: University Press of Mississippi, 1984.

Marsh, Charles. *God's Long Summer: Stories of Faith and Civil Rights.* Princeton: Princeton University Press, 1997.

Meacham, Jon, ed. *Voices in Our Blood: America's Best on the Civil Rights Movement.* New York: Random House, 2001.

Meier, August, and Elliott Rudwick. *CORE: A Study of the Civil Rights Movement, 1942–1968.* Urbana: University of Illinois Press, 1975.

Meier, August, John Bracey, Jr. and Elliot Rudwick, eds. *Black Pro-test in the Sixties.* New York: Markus Wiener, Publishers, 1991.

Morgan, Iwan, and Philip Davies, eds. *From Sit-ins to SNCC: The Student Civil Rights Movement in the 1960s.* Tallahassee: University Press of Florida, 2012.

Morris, Aldon D. *The Origins of the Civil Rights Movement: Black Communities Organizing for Change.* New York: The Free Press, 1984.

Moye, J. Todd. *Ella Baker: Community Organizer of the Civil Rights Movement.* Lanham: Rowman & Littlefield Publishers, Inc., 2013.

Murray, Paul T. *The Civil Rights Movement: References and Resources.* New York: G. K. Hall, 1993.

Olson, Lynne. *Freedom's Daughters: The Unsung Heroines of the Civil Rights Movement from 1830 to 1970.* New York: Scribner, 2001.

Oppenheimer, Martin. *The Sit-in Movement of 1960.* Brooklyn: Carlson Publishing, 1989.

Payne, Charles M. *I've Got the Light of Freedom: The Organizing Tradition and the Mississippi Freedom Struggle.* Berkeley: University of California Press, 1995.

Pfeffer, Paula F. *A. Philip Randolph: Pioneer of the Civil Rights Movement.* Baton Rouge: Louisiana State University Press, 1990.

Powledge, Fred. *Free at Last?: The Civil Rights Movement and the People Who Made It.* New York: Harper Perennial, 1992.

Ransby, Barbara. *Ella Baker and the Black Freedom Movement: A Radical Democratic Vision.* Chapel Hill: University of North Carolina Press, 2003.

Romano, Renee C., and Leigh Raiford, eds. *The Civil Rights Movement in American Memory.* Athens: University of Georgia Press, 2006.

Scanlon, Jennifer. *Until There Is Justice: The Life of Anna Arnold Hedgeman.* New York: Oxford University Press, 2016.

Sugrue, Thomas J. *Sweet Land of Liberty: The Forgotten Struggle for Civil Rights in the North.* New York: Random House, 2008.

Sullivan, Patricia. *Lift Every Voice: The NAACP and the Making of the Civil Rights Movement.* New York: New Press, 2009.

Weisbrot, Robert. *Freedom Bound: A History of America's Civil Rights Movement.* New York: W. W. Norton & Company, 1990.

Weiss, Nancy J. *Whitney M. Young, Jr., and the Struggle for Civil Rights.* Princeton, NJ: Princeton University Press, 1990.

Williams, Juan. *Eyes on the Prize: America's Civil Rights Years, 1954–1965.* New York: Viking, 1987.

Witcover, Jules. *The Year the Dream Died: Revisiting 1968 in America.* New York: Warner Books, 1997.

Zinn, Howard. *SNCC: The New Abolitionists.* Boston: Beacon Press, 1964.

CIVIL RIGHTS MOVEMENT (PHOTOGRAPHIC HISTORY)

Adelman, Bob, and Charles Johnson. *Mine Eyes Have Seen: Bearing Witness to the Struggle for Civil Rights.* (Live Great Photographers Series). New York: Time, Inc., Home Entertainment Books, 2007.

Berger, Martin A. *Freedom Now!: Forgotten Photographs of the Civil Rights Struggle.* Berkeley: University of California Press, 2013.

Cobb, Charles E. *This Light of Ours: Activist Photographers of the Civil Rights Movement.* Jackson: University Press of Mississippi, 2012.

Counts, Will; Will Campbell, Ernest Dumas, and Robert S. McCord. *A Life Is More Than a Moment: The Desegregation of Little Rock's Central High.* Bloomington: Indiana University Press, 1999.

Cox, Julian, *Road to Freedom: Photographs of the Civil Rights Movement, 1956–1968.* Atlanta: High Museum of Art, 2008.

Cox, Julian, Rebekah Jacobs, and Monica Karales. *Controversy and Hope: The Civil Rights Photographs of James Karales.* Columbia: The University of South Carolina Press, 2013.

Davidson, Bruce. *Time of Change: Civil Rights Photographs, 1961–1965*. Los Angeles: St. Ann's Press, 2002.

Durham, Michael S. *Powerful Days: The Civil Rights Photographs of Charles Moore*. Tuscaloosa: University of Alabama Press, 1991.

Baldwin, Frederick C. *Freedom's March: Photographs of the Civil Rights Movement in Savannah by Frederick C. Baldwin*. Savannah: Telfair Museum of Art, 2008.

Lyon, Danny. *Memories of the Southern Civil Rights Movement*. Chapel Hill: University of North Carolina Press, 1992.

Raiford, Leigh. *Imprisoned in a Luminous Glare: Photography and the African American Freedom Struggle*. Chapel Hill: University of North Carolina Press, 2011.

Randell, Herbert, and Bobs M. Tusa. *Faces of Freedom Summer*. Tuscaloosa: University of Alabama Press, 2001.

CIVIL RIGHTS MOVEMENT (FOCUS ON SPECIFIC INCIDENTS—OTHER SOURCES)

THE MONTGOMERY BUS BOYCOTT

Brinkley, Douglas. *Rosa Parks*. New York: Viking, 2000.

Garrow, David J., ed. *The Walking City: The Montgomery Bus Boycott, 1955–1956*. Brooklyn: Carlson Publishing, 1969.

Leventhal, Willy S. *The Children Coming On: A Retrospective of the Montgomery Bus Boycott*. Montgomery: Black Belt Press, 1968.

Theoharis, Jeanne. *The Rebellious Life of Mrs. Rosa Parks*. Boston: Beacon Press, 2013.

Williams, Donnie, and Wayne Greenhaw. *The Thunder of Angels: The Montgomery Bus Boycott and the People Who Broke the Back of Jim Crow*. Chicago: Lawrence Hill Books, 2006.

16TH STREET BAPTIST CHURCH BOMBING

Cobbs, Elizabeth H., and Petric J. Smith. *Long Time Coming: An Insider's Story of the Birmingham Church Bombing That Rocked the World*. Birmingham: Crane Hill, 1994.

Federal Bureau of Investigation vault website: https://vault.fbi.gov /16th%20Street%20Church%20Bombing%20 (in 50 parts)

Sikora, Frank. *Until Justice Rolls Down: The Birmingham Church Bombing Case.* Tuscaloosa: University of Alabama Press, 1991.

MISSISSIPPI BURNING (THE KILLING OF THREE CIVIL RIGHTS WORKERS)

Ball, Howard. *Justice in Mississippi: The Murder Trial of Edgar Ray Killen.* Lawrence: University Press of Kansas, 2008.

———. *Murder in Mississippi:* United States v. Price *and the Struggle for Civil Rights.* Lawrence: University Press of Kansas, 2004.

Cagin, Seth, and Phillip Drey. *We Are Not Afraid: The Story of Goodman, Schwerner, and Chaney and the Civil Rights Campaign for Mississippi.* New York: Macmillan, 1988.

Federal Bureau of Investigation vault website: https://vault.fbi.gov /Mississippi%20Burning%20(MIBURN)%20Case (in 9 parts)

Huie, William Bradford. *Three Lives for Mississippi*, 2nd edition with introduction by Martin Luther King, Jr. New York: New American Library, 1968.

U.S. Department of Justice. Report to the Attorney General of the State of Mississippi. *Investigation of the 1964 Murders of Michael*

Schwerner, James Chaney, and Andrew Goodman. Washington, DC: U.S. Department of Justice, Civil Rights Division, 2016: http://www.ago.state.ms.us/wp-content/uploads/2016/06/DOJ-Report-to-Mississippi-Attorney-General-Jim-Hood.pdf.

Watson, Bruce. *Freedom Summer: The Savage Season of 1964 That Made Mississippi Burn and Made America a Democracy.* New York: Viking Press, 2010

THE MARCH ON WASHINGTON, 1963

Euchner, Charles C. *Nobody Turn Me Around: A People's History of the 1963 March on Washington.* Boston: Beacon Press, 2010.

Freed, Leonard, photographer. *This Is the Day: The March on Washington.* Los Angeles: J. Paul Getty Museum, 2013.

Gentile, Thomas. *March on Washington, August 28, 1963.* Washington, DC: New Day Publications, 1983.

Hansen, Drew D. *The Dream: Martin Luther King, Jr., and the Speech That Inspired a Nation.* New York: HarperCollins Publishers, 2003.

Jones, William P. *March on Washington: Jobs, Freedom and the Forgotten History of the Civil Rights Movement.* New York: W. W. Norton & Company, 2013.

Kelly, Kitty. *Let Freedom Ring: Stanley Tretlick's Iconic Images of the March on Washington*. New York: St. Martin's Press, 2013.

SELMA: VOTING RIGHTS

Fager, Charles. *Selma, 1965*. New York: Scribner, 1974. Several revised and updated editions with more photos as *Selma, 1965: The March That Changed the South*.

Garrow, David J. *Protest at Selma: Martin Luther King, Jr., and the Voting Rights Act of 1965*. New Haven, CT: Yale University Press, 1978.

Mills, Thornton J., III. *Dividing Lines: Municipal Politics and the Struggle for Civil Rights in Montgomery and Selma*. Tuscaloosa: University of Alabama Press, 2002.

CIVIL RIGHTS MOVEMENT (POLITICAL ASPECTS—STATES, CONGRESS, THE PRESIDENT, AND THE EXECUTIVE BRANCH)

Berman, William C. *The Politics of Civil Rights in the Truman Administration.* Columbus: Ohio State University Press, 1970.

Berry, Mary Frances. *And Justice for All: The United States Commission on Civil Rights and the Continuing Struggle for Freedom in America.* New York: Alfred A. Knopf, 2009.

Black, Earl. *Southern Governors and Civil Rights.* Cambridge, MA: Harvard University Press, 1976.

Brauer, Carl M. *John F. Kennedy and the Second Reconstruction.* New York: Columbia University Press, 1977.

Bryant, Nick. *The Bystander: John F. Kennedy and the Struggle for Black Equality.* New York: Basic Books, 2006.

Burk, Robert Frederick. *The Eisenhower Administration and Black Civil Rights.* Knoxville: University of Tennessee Press, 1984.

Gardner, Michael R. *Harry Truman and Civil Rights: Moral Courage and Political Risks*. Carbondale: Southern Illinois University Press, 2002.

Golden, Harry. *Mr. Kennedy and the Negroes*. Cleveland: World Publishing, 1964.

Graham, Hugh Davis. *Civil Rights and the Presidency: Race and Gender in American Politics, 1960–1972*. New York: Oxford University Press, 1992.

Kotz, Nick. *Judgment Days: Lyndon Baines Johnson, Martin Luther King Jr., and the Laws That Changed America*. Boston: Houghton Mifflin, 2005.

McCoy, Donald, and Richard T. Reuten. *Quest and Response: Minority Rights and the Truman Administration*. Lawrence: University of Kansas Press, 1988.

McKee, Guian A., Kent B. Germany, David C. Carter, and Timothy Naftali, eds. *The Presidential Recordings: Lyndon B. Johnson, Mississippi Burning and the Passage of the Civil Rights Act, June 1, 1964–July 4, 1964*. Volumes 7 and 8. New York: W. W. Norton, 2011.

Mann, Robert. *When Freedom Would Triumph: The Civil Rights Struggle in Congress, 1954–1968*. Baton Rouge: Louisiana State University Press, 2007.

———. *The Walls of Jericho: Lyndon Johnson, Hubert Humphrey, Richard Russell, and the Struggle for Civil Rights*. New York: Harcourt Brace, 1996.

Mills, Thornton J., III, *Dividing Lines: Municipal Politics and the Struggle for Civil Rights in Montgomery and Selma*. Tuscaloosa: University of Alabama Press, 2002.

Nicols, David A. *A Matter of Justice: Eisenhower and the Beginning of the Civil Rights Revolution*. New York: Simon & Schuster, 2007.

Niven, David. *The Politics of Injustice: The Kennedys, the Freedom Rides, and the Electoral Consequences of Moral Compromise*. Knoxville: University of Tennessee Press, 2003.

Rosenberg, Jonathan, and Zachery Karabell. *Kennedy, Johnson, and the Quest for Justice: The Civil Rights Tapes*. New York: W. W. Norton, 2003.

Stern, Mark. *Calculating Visions: Kennedy, Johnson, and Civil Rights*. New Brunswick: Rutgers University Press, 1992.

Wolk, Allan. *The Presidency and Black Civil Rights: Eisenhower to Nixon*. Rutherford: Fairleigh Dickinson University Press, 1971.

KING'S FINAL DAYS (MEMPHIS STRIKE)

Bailey, D'Army. *Mine Eyes Have Seen: Dr. Martin Luther King Jr.'s Final Journey.* Memphis: Towery Publishing, 1993.

Honey, Michael K. *Going Down Jericho Road: The Memphis Strike, Martin Luther King's Last Campaign.* New York: W. W. Norton & Company, 2007.

Smiley, Tavis, with David Riz. *The Death of a King: The Real Story of Dr. Martin Luther King Jr.'s Final Year.* New York: Little, Brown, 2014.

Withers, Ernest C. *I Am a Man: Photographs of the 1968 Memphis Sanitation Strike and Martin Luther King, Jr.* Memphis, TN: Memphis Publishing, 1993.

Also, the website of the American Federation of State, County, and Municipal Employees (AFSCME): http://www.afscme.org /union/history/mlk and http://www.afscme.org/union/history /mlk/1968-afscme-memphis-sanitation-workers-strike-chronology

THE CIVIL RIGHTS ORGANIZATIONS

Congress of Racial Equality (CORE): http://www.congressofracial equality.org and http://www.core-online.org

National Association for the Advancement of Colored People (NAACP): http://www.naacp.org

National Urban League: http://nul.iamempowered.com

Southern Christian Leadership Conference (SCLC): http:// nationalsclc.org

Student Nonviolent Coordinating Committee (SNCC). The organization no longer exists, but see http://www.sncclegacyproject.org

BLACK POWER MOVEMENT: BLACK MUSLIMS, BLACK PANTHERS, AND OTHERS (PRIMARY SOURCES)

Carmichael, Stokely, and Charles V. Hamilton. *Black Power: The Struggle of Liberation in America*. New York: Random House, 1967.

Carmichael, Stokely, with Ekwueme Michael Thelwell. *Ready for Revolution: The Life and Struggles of Stokely Carmichael (Kwame Ture).* New York: Scribner, 2003.

Cleaver, Eldridge. *Soul on Ice.* New York: McGraw-Hill, 1968.

———. *Soul on Fire.* Waco, TX: Word Books, 1978.

Davis, Angela. *Angela Davis: An Autobiography.* New York: Random House, 1974.

Foner, Philip S., ed. *The Black Panthers Speak.* Philadelphia: J. P. Lippincott, 1970.

Muhammad, Elijah. *Message to the Black Man in America.* Chicago: Elijah Muhammad House of Islam, 1965.

Heath, G. Louis, ed. *The Black Panther Leaders Speak: Huey P. Newton, Bobby Seale, Eldridge Cleaver, and Company Speak through the Black Panther Party Official Newspaper.* Metuchen: Scarecrow Press, 1976.

Malcolm X. *The Autobiography of Malcolm X, as told to Alex Haley.* New York: Grove Press, 1966.

Newton, Huey P. *To Die for the People.* New York: Random House, 1972.

Newton, Huey P., and J. Herman Blake. *Revolutionary Suicide.* New York: Harcourt Brace Jovanovich, 1973.

Seale, Bobby. *A Lonely Rage: The Autobiography of Bobby Seale.* New York: Times Books, 1978.

————. *Seize the Time: The Story of the Black Panther Party and Huey P. Newton.* New York: Random House, 1970.

Sellers, Cleveland, and Robert Terrell. *The River of No Return: The Autobiography of a Black Militant and the Life and Death of SNCC.* New York: William Morrow, 1973.

BLACK POWER MOVEMENT (GENERAL SOURCES)

Austin, Curtis J. *Up Against the Wall: Violence in the Making and Unmaking of the Black Panther Party.* Fayetteville: University of Arkansas Press, 2006.

Bloom, Joshua. *Black Against Empire: The History and Politics of the Black Panther Party.* Berkeley: University of California Press, 2013.

Cleaver, Kathleen, and George Katsiaficas. *Liberation, Imagination, and the Black Panther Party: A New Look at the Panthers and Their Legacy.* New York: Routledge, 2001.

Haines, Herbert. *Black Radicals and the Civil Rights Mainstream, 1954–1970.* Knoxville: University of Tennessee Press, 1988.

Joseph, Peniel E. *Waiting 'Til the Midnight Hour: A Narrative of the History of Black Power in America.* New York: Henry Holt, 2006.

Lomax, Louis E. *When the Word Is Given . . . : A Report on Elijah Muhammad, Malcolm X, and the Black Muslim World.* Cleveland: World Publishing, 1963.

Pearson, Hugh. *The Shadow of the Panther: Huey Newton and the Price of Black Power in America.* Reading, MA: Addison-Wesley Publishing, 1994.

Van Deburg, William L. *New Day in Babylon: The Black Power Movement in American Culture, 1965–1975.* Chicago: University of Chicago Press, 1992.

"BLACK POWER" WEBSITES

The Black Panthers: http://theblackpanthers.com/home/

Nation of Islam (formerly called the Black Muslims): http://www
.noi.org

KING ASSASSINATION AND AFTERMATH (NON-CONSPIRACY WORKS)

Ayton, Mel. *A Racial Crime: James Earl Ray and the Murder of Martin Luther King.* Las Vegas: Arche Books Publishing, 2005

Blair, Clay, Jr. *The Strange Case of James Earl Ray: The Man Who Murdered Martin Luther King.* New York: Bantam Books, 1979.

Burns, Rebecca. *Burial for a King: Martin Luther King Jr.'s Funeral and the Week That Transformed Atlanta and Rocked the Nation.* New York: Scribner, 2011.

Clarke, James W. *American Assassins: The Darker Side of American Politics.* Princeton: Princeton University Press, 1982.

Frank, Gerold. *An American Death: The True Story of the Assassination of Dr. Martin Luther King, Jr. and the Greatest Manhunt of Our Time.* Garden City: Doubleday, 1972.

Gilbert, Ben W., and the staff of the *Washington Post. Ten Blocks from the White House: Anatomy of the Washington Riots of 1968.* New York: F. A. Praeger, 1968.

Huie, William Bradford. *He Slew the Dreamer: My Search for the Truth about James Earl Ray and the Murder of Martin Luther King.* New York: Delacorte Press, 1970. Later published in 1977 with a more alluring and enticing title, *Did the FBI Kill Martin Luther King?*

James Earl Ray: The Man and the Mystery. A&E Television Network, 1998. 50 minutes (DVD).

The James Earl Ray Extradition File: Papers Submitted to Great Britain for the Extradition of James Earl Ray to Face Trial for the Murder of Martin Luther King, Jr. New York: Lemma Publishing, 1971.

Justice for MLK: The Hunt for James Earl Ray. Cream Productions, in association with the American Heroes Channel (AHC), 2016. 58 minutes (documentary).

Kamin, Ben. *Room 306: The National Story of the Lorraine Motel.* Lansing: Michigan State University Press, 2012.

Lomax, Louis E. *To Kill a Black Man: The Shocking Parallel in the Lives of Malcolm X and Martin Luther King.* Los Angeles: Holloway House, 1968.

McMillan, George. *The Making of an Assassin: The Life of James Earl Ray.* Boston: Little, Brown, 1976.

MLK: The Assassination Tapes. Smithsonian Channel, 2012. 46 minutes. (DVD)

Obsequies Martin Luther King, Jr.: Tuesday, April 9, 1968, 10:30 A.M. Ebenezer Baptist Church, 2:00 P.M. The Campus of Morehouse College, Atlanta, Georgia. No publisher, 1968. (twelve-page funeral program)

Posner, Gerald. *Killing the Dream: James Earl Ray and the Assassination of Martin Luther King, Jr.* New York: Random House, 1998.

Risen, Clay. *A Nation on Fire: America in the Wake of the King Assassination.* Hoboken, NJ: John Wiley & Sons, 2009.

Roads to Memphis: Two Paths, One Ending (American Experience Series). Public Broadcasting Service (PBS), 2010. 90 minutes (documentary).

Ryan, P. L. *The Boys of Birmingham.* N.p.: Jimerson Publishing Company, 2009.

Seigenthaler, John. *A Search for Justice.* Nashville, TN: Aurora Publishers, 1971.

Shelby County Register of Deeds. *Dr. Martin Luther King, Jr. Assassination Investigation.* A comprehensive resource of the investigation, evidence, court record, trial, etc. can be found at http://register.shelby.tn.us/media/mlk/

Sides, Hampton. *Hellhound on His Trail: The Stalking of Martin Luther King, Jr. and the International Hunt for His Assassin.* New York: Doubleday Garden City, 2010.

U.S. Department of Justice. *Report of the Department of Justice Task Force to Review the FBI Martin Luther King, Jr. Security and Assassination Investigation.* Washington, DC: The Task Force, 1977, https://vault.fbi.gov/Martin%20Luther%20King%2C%20Jr./Martin%20Luther%20King%2C%20Jr.%20Part%201%20of%202/view

U.S. Department of Justice. *Investigation of Recent Allegations Regarding the Assassination of Dr. Martin Luther King, Jr.* Washington, DC: Department of Justice, June 2000. Refuting the jury's verdict in *King v. Jowers*, a civil suit in Tennessee state court that found that Loyd Jowers, a former Memphis tavern owner, and unnamed individuals, including unspecified government agencies, participated in the conspiracy to assassinate Dr. King: https://www.justice.gov/crt/united-states-department-justice-investigation-recent-allegations-regarding-assassination-dr; and https://www.justice.gov/crt/list-attachments-0

U.S. House of Representatives. *Select Committee on Assassinations.* (13 volumes, "The Investigation of the Assassination of Martin Luther King," and 1 volume "Final Report"). 95th Congress, 2nd Session. Washington, DC: Government Printing Office, 1979. This report is available online at http://www.maryferrell.org/pages/Martin_Luther _King_Assassination.html

U.S. House of Representatives. *Select Committee on Assassinations.* "Staff Report—Compilation of the Statements of James Earl Ray." 95th Congress, 2nd Session. Washington, DC: Government Printing Office, 1978.

Whosoever: Metropolitan Interdenominational Church; "Citizens of the World"; Metro—A Service of the Death and Resurrection; In Memoriam, James Earl Ray, May 28, 1998. Nashville, Tennessee. (4-page James Earl Ray funeral program)

KING ASSASSINATION (CONSPIRACY WORKS)

Blumenthal, Sid, and Harvey Yazijian, eds. *Government by Gunplay: Assassination Conspiracy Theories from Dallas to Today.* New York: New American Library, 1976.

Committee to Investigate Assassinations. *American Political Assassinations: A Bibliography of Works Published 1963–1970, Relating to the Assassinations of John F. Kennedy, Martin Luther King, Robert F. Kennedy.* Washington, DC: Special Collections Division, Georgetown University Library, 1973. Several versions of this were published. This was Bud Fensterwald/Jim Lasar's effort, which later became the Assassination Archives and Research Center.

Conspiracy?: Who Killed Martin Luther King, Jr. History Channel, original aired in 2003, 45 minutes. Now part of a 3-DVD set: https://www.youtube.com/watch?v=uY3mszZlebo

DiEugenio, James, and Lisa Pease, eds. *The Assassinations: Probe Magazine on JFK, MLK, RFK, and Malcolm X.* Los Angeles: Feral House, 2003.

Dyson, Michael Eric. *April 4, 1968: Martin Luther King Jr.'s Death and How It Changed America.* New York: Basic Civitas Books, 2008.

Emison, John Avery. *The Martin Luther King Congressional Cover-Up: The Railroading of James Earl Ray, LA.* Gretna: Pelican Publishing, 2014.

Gabriel, Michael. *James Earl Ray: The Last Days of Inmate #65477.* Los Angeles: Cat Yoga Publishing, 2004.

"The King Murder Mystery: Will a New Investigation Establish the Truth?" *Skeptic: The Magazine of Opposing View*, 18 (March/April 1977).

King v. Jowers (trial transcript): http://www.thekingcenter.org/sites /default/files/KING%20FAMILY%20TRIAL%20TRANSCRIPT .pdf

Lane, Mark, and Dick Gregory. *Code Name "Zorro": The Murder of Martin Luther King, Jr.* Englewood Cliffs: Prentice-Hall, 1977. Reprinted in 1993 as *Murder in Memphis.*

McMichael, Pate. *Klandestine: How a Klan Lawyer and a Checkbook Journalist Helped James Earl Ray.* Chicago: Chicago Review Press, 2015.

Marks, Stanley. *Coup D'Etat: November 22, 1963; The Conspiracies That Murdered President Kennedy, the Rev. Martin Luther King, and Senator Robert F. Kennedy with Comments of the Trials of Clay B. Shaw, Sirhan B. Sirhan, and James Earl Ray.* Los Angeles: Bureau of International Affairs, 1970.

Melanson, Philip H. *The Murkin Conspiracy: An Investigation into the Assassination of Dr. Martin Luther King, Jr.* New York: Praeger, 1989.

————. *Who Killed Martin Luther King?* (The Real Story Series). Berkeley: Odonian Press, 1993.

Melanson, Philip H., and Noah Griffin. *The Martin Luther King Assassination: New Revelations on the Conspiracy and Cover-Up, 1968–1991.* New York: Shapolsky Publishers, 1994.

Newton, Michael. *A Case for Conspiracy.* Los Angeles: Holloway House Publishing, 1980. Reprinted in 1987 as *The King Conspiracy.*

Pepper, William F. *An Act of State: The Execution of Martin Luther King.* New York: Verso, 2008.

————. *Orders to Kill: The Truth behind the Murder of Martin Luther King, Jr.* New York: Warner Books, 1998. Revised, updated, and expanded as *The Plot to Kill the King: The Truth behind the Assassination of Martin Luther King, Jr.* New York: Skyhorse Publishing, 2016.

Potash, John. *The FBI War on Tupac Shakur and Black Leaders: U.S. Intelligence's Murderous Targeting of Tupac, MLK, Malcolm, Panthers, Hendrix, Marley, Rappers & Linked Ethnic Leftists.* s.l.: Progressive Left Press, 2008.

Ray, James Earl. *Tennessee Waltz: The Making of a Political Prisoner.* Saint Andrews: Saint Andrews Press, 1987.

————. *Who Killed Martin Luther King?: The True Story by the Alleged Assassin.* Washington, DC: National Press Books, 1992.

Ray, Jerry, and Tamara Carter. *A Memoir of Injustice: By the Younger Brother of James Earl Ray, Alleged Assassin of Martin Luther King, Jr.* Walterville: TrineDay, 2011.

Ray, John Larry, and Lyndon Barsten. *Truth at Last: The Untold Story behind James Earl Ray and the Assassination of Martin Luther King, Jr.* Guilford: Lyons Press, 2008.

Ross, Robert Gaylon. *The Elite Serial Killers of Lincoln, JFK, RFK & MLK.* Spicewood: RIE, 2001.

Savastano, Carmine. *Two Princes and a King: A Concise Review of Three Political Assassinations.* Neapolis Media Group, 2016.

Scott, Peter Dale, Paul L. Hoch, and Russell Stetler. *The Assassinations: Dallas and Beyond: A Guide to Cover-ups and Investigations.* New York: Random House, 1976.

The Murder of Dr. Martin Luther King, Jr. African American History Network. (2 DVDs)

The 13th Juror: The Official Transcript of the Martin Luther King Assassination Conspiracy Trial. s.l.: MLK the Truth, LLC, 2009.

Weisberg, Harold. *Frame-Up: The Martin Luther King/James Earl Ray Case Containing Suppressed Evidence.* New York: Outerbridge & Dienstfrey, 1971. Several reprints, such as *Martin Luther King: The Assassination.* New York: Carroll & Graf, 1993. (with a postscript by James Earl Ray)

Wexler, Stuart, and Larry Hancock. *The Awful Grace of God: Religion, Terrorism, White Supremacy, and the Unsolved Murder of Martin Luther King, Jr.* Berkeley: Counterpoint, 2012.

Who Killed Martin Luther King, Jr.? Clarendon Ent., 2008. 64 minutes, (DVD).

Wilson, Donald G. *Evidence Withheld: The True Story of the FBI Cover-Up in the Assassination of the Rev. Martin Luther King. Jr.* Parker: Outskirts Press, 2013.

KING (FBI MONITORING)

Churchill, Ward, and Jim Vander Wall. *The COINTELPRO Papers: Documents from the FBI's Secret War against Domestic Dissent.* Boston: South End Press, 1990.

Friedly, Michael, and David Gallen. *Martin Luther King., Jr.: The FBI File.* New York: Carroll & Graf, 1993.

Garrow, David J. *The FBI and Martin Luther King, Jr., from "Solo" to Memphis.* New York: W. W. Norton & Company, 1981.

Johnson, Loch K. *Season of Inquiry: The Senate Intelligence Investigation.* Lexington: University of Kentucky Press, 1985.

McKnight, Gerald. *The Last Crusade: Martin Luther King Jr., the FBI, and the Poor People's Campaign.* Boulder, CO: Westview Press, 1998.

O'Reilly, Kenneth. *Black Americans: The FBI Files.* New York: Carroll & Graf, 1994.

————. *Racial Matters: The FBI's Secret File on Black America, 1960–1972.* New York: The Free Press, 1992.

U.S. Senate. *Supplemental Detailed Staff Reports on Intelligence Activities and the Rights of Americans.* Final Report of the Select Committee to Study Governmental Operations with Respect to Intelligence Activities. 94th Congress, 2nd Session, Senate Report 94-755. Washington, DC: Government Printing Office, April 23, 1976. Book III ("the Church Committee"). (This volume is specifically related to FBI, COINTELPRO, and Martin Luther King, Jr.: http://www.aarclibrary.org/publib/church/reports/book3/html/ChurchB3_0001a.htm)

U.S. Senate. *Hearings: Federal Bureau of Investigation.* Select Committee to Study Governmental Operations with Respect to Intelligence Activities. 94th Congress, 1st Session. Washington, DC: Government Printing Office, 1976. Volume VI ("the Church Committee").

U.S., 109th Congress, 2nd Session, House-Senate Companion Bills, H.R. 2554 and S. 2499, the Martin Luther King, Jr. Records Collection Act of 2006, a bill to create a Records Review Board to collect all government records relating to Martin Luther King. No Congressional action. Sen. John Kerry (D-MA) and Rep. John Lewis (D-GA) announced plans to reintroduce the legislation in the 112th Congress in 2010, but it was not introduced.

Note: Page numbers in *italics* refer to illustrations.

CREDITS AND PERMISSIONS

Library of Congress Cataloging-in-Publication Data

Names: Swanson, James L., 1959- author.
Title: Chasing King's killer : the hunt for Martin Luther King, Jr.'s assassin / by James L. Swanson.
Other titles: Hunt for Martin Luther King, Jr.'s assassin
Description: First edition. | New York : Scholastic Press, [2018] | Includes bibliographical references and index. | Audience: Grades 9-12. | Audience: Age 12 and up.
Identifiers: LCCN 2017008562 | ISBN 9780545723336 (hardcover : alk.paper)
Subjects: LCSH: King, Martin Luther, Jr., 1929-1968—Assassination—Juvenile literature. | Ray, James Earl, 1928-1998—Juvenile literature.
Classification: LCC E185.97.K5 S95 2018 | DDC 323.092 [B]—dc23 LC record available at https://lccn.loc.gov/2017008562

10 9 8 7 6 5 4 3 2 1   18 19 20 21 22

Maps and diagrams: Illustrations by Steve Stankiewicz on pages 143, 152-153 and Illustrations by Jim McMahon on pages 103, 133, 234 © Scholastic Inc.

Printed in the U.S.A. 23

First edition, January 2018

The display type was set in AgencyFB.
The text was set in Adobe Garamond Pro.

Book design by Phil Falco

Chasing King's Killer is my fourth book for young adults, and it is the final installment in my trilogy on the lives, last days, and assassinations of three American heroes: Abraham Lincoln, John F. Kennedy, and Martin Luther King, Jr.

My wife, Andrea E. Mays, provided encouragement and, most importantly, valuable editorial assistance and a careful and perceptive reading of several versions of the manuscript. This is a story about one of the bravest, most courageous men in American history, yet it would have to end in tragedy and heartbreak. Andrea kept me focused on the fact that this is not just a book about a sad and tragic death, but about a great life.

The incomparable David Lovett, lawyer, historian, and bibliographer on American political assassinations, made many valuable contributions. From his huge library—the best in the country—on the murders of Kennedy, Lincoln, and King, he loaned me many rare items. David scrutinized and improved the manuscript, bibliography, and notes with expert eyes. I also thank my good friend Lucas Morel, Professor of Politics at Washington and Lee University, for a careful and thoughtful reading of the manuscript.

Erica Munkwitz, a professor of history at American University, provided indispensable research and editorial advice. A scholar of the

British Empire, Erica is a talented writer and discerning editor, with a natural storytelling gift and instinct for dramatic detail. Not only did she add a fresh and compelling perspective to the narrative, but she also discovered several rare photos that proved essential to telling the story in images as well as words. At the same time, Erica helped save me from getting bogged down in the weeds by admonishing me not to overload the book with too much arcane minutiae that, while fascinating to me, would interrupt the story's momentum and not engage young readers.

The Achilles' heel of anyone who writes about history is the temptation to assume that you always need more and more facts, and that if you just accumulate enough of them, you will always find the answers. Perhaps the most frustrating yet alluring thing about history is that its mysteries sometimes defy explanation, and we cannot always discover the answer to every question.

I thank my friend Dan McCarthy for photographing Martin Luther King, Jr., artifacts that appear in this book. Dan's enthusiasm and support for this project was contagious.

My agent, Richard Abate, is also a passionate historian in his own right and his judicious advice helped steer this book on the right course. This is our seventh book together, and he has—as always—acted as a trusted advisor, confidante, and friend.

Congressman John Lewis, with whom I am proud to serve on the Advisory Council of the Ford's Theatre Society, was kind enough to contribute the foreword to this book. A heroic veteran of the civil rights movement, Congressman Lewis not only lived through history, he helped to make it.

I thank my friend Congressman Joe Crowley for his wise counsel and personal assistance throughout this project. Congressman Crowley has a true sense of history, and I have benefited from our many conversations about the American story.

I also thank the late Julian Bond for a memorable conversation about the King assassination that we had at Ford's Theatre on the night of April 14, 2015, the 150th anniversary of the assassination of Abraham Lincoln. And I thank Dorothy Nash, another great veteran of the movement, for encouraging words.

Two men inspired me to write this book. My father, Lennart Swanson, set it in motion when he came home from work on April 5, 1968, the day after King's assassination. He was the president of the Maurice Lenell Cookie Company, a beloved Chicago institution, and he told me that many of his employees had asked him if they could leave work early that day. In the aftermath of the assassination, riots and fires had broken out in their neighborhoods on the south and west sides of Chicago and they wanted to go home to protect their families. Together my father and I, just age nine, watched the rioting and fires on the television news. Later, when it was all over, my father drove me through the ruins. He wanted me to see history with my own eyes, and to remember it. It took decades for parts of my city to recover from the King assassination.

This book also takes me back to some of my earliest, formative childhood memories. I remember the funeral of President John F. Kennedy; the assassination of his brother, Senator Robert Kennedy; the Vietnam War; and the Apollo space program—and I also remember Martin Luther King, Jr. Every evening, I watched the network evening news with my parents, and I remember the coverage of Dr.

King's visit to Chicago in 1966, how he was greeted with hatred. I also recall that some of my elementary school classmates (no doubt repeating what they heard at home) said cruel things about King. And I watched television coverage of his assassination. Later on, at our local post office, I saw the FBI wanted posters for James Earl Ray—the same ones that you now see in this book—displayed inside a locked glass case hanging on the wall. Today, not far from my home in Washington, DC, the Martin Luther King, Jr. Memorial stands tall when I drive past it at night. King could not have imagined it: a colossal statue of himself within sight of the Lincoln Memorial, the location of his triumphant speech in August 1963, and not far from the Vietnam War Memorial, the conflict he had hoped to end.

The other man who inspired me to tell this story is John Hope Franklin, my professor, mentor, and friend at the University of Chicago. John Hope was a titanic figure. His landmark book, *From Slavery to Freedom*, as well as his other writings, made the compelling case that African American history is a vital and central part of the American experience and must not be shunted aside and studied in isolation. In his field, he was the best there ever was. And he was one of the finest men I have ever known. Since his death in March 2009 at age 94, I've come to realize even more how much he has influenced my literary choices and understanding of the past.

My wonderful editor, Dianne Hess, shares my vivid memories of the tumultuous 1960s. From our first meeting, we recognized what a profound and emotional impact that the decade had on us, especially the stories of John F. Kennedy and Martin Luther King, Jr. This book takes us back to the shared experiences and memories from our childhoods. We hope that, in addition to telling the story of Dr. King's last days, the book transports readers back in time and gives them a feeling of what it was like to be alive in 1960s America. Dianne's passion for the subject, her sense of story, and her editorial skill made this a more engaging story. I have fond memories of us standing around my dining room table and sorting through piles of photographs as we discussed each image we wanted to include in the book. Our mutual obsession to find just the right images to advance the story made this a better book. I thank her for indulging me on numerous occasions when I pleaded, "Can't we include just one more picture?"

I thank my other friends at Scholastic, too. Ellie Berger, president of Trade Publishing, has offered generous support for all of my books. When I was a boy, I eagerly awaited the arrival of the latest Scholastic book club catalog so I could order the newest history titles. Now we have published three books together, with more to come. Tracy van Straaten, vice president of publicity and marketing, works hard to make sure that my work reaches the widest possible audience, as does my publicist, Lauren Donovan. The talented and amazing Phil Falco did a beautiful job creating the cover and the layout. This is my third book that Phil has designed, and he has outdone himself every time.

Finally, I thank you, my readers, for your interest in my books. I have enjoyed reading your letters and meeting many of you at events across the country. I hope to visit your school someday to speak about reading, storytelling, and history.

JAMES L. SWANSON
WASHINGTON, DC

JAMES L. SWANSON is the author of the *New York Times* best-sellers *Manhunt: The 12-Day Chase for Lincoln's Killer* and its sequel, *Bloody Crimes: The Chase for Jefferson Davis and the Death Pageant for Lincoln's Corpse. Manhunt* won the Edgar Award for best nonfiction crime book of the year. James's page-turning, you-are-there, historic crime dramas include the bestselling classic *Chasing Lincoln's Killer*, an adaptation of *Manhunt* for young readers, which has more than one million copies in print. He also penned *Bloody Times*, the young adult version of *Bloody Crimes*. His pictorial book *Lincoln's Assassins: Their Trial and Execution* is an acclaimed photo history of the crime, the pursuit of the conspirators, and their fates. He also wrote about the assassination of President John F. Kennedy in his award-winning young adult book, *"The President Has Been Shot!": The Assassination of John F. Kennedy* as well as the adult version, *End of Days: The Assassination of John F. Kennedy*. He was a recipient of a Historic Deerfield Fellowship in Early American History, and he serves on the advisory councils of the Ford's Theatre Society and the Gettysburg Foundation. He also serves on the board of the Abraham Lincoln Association. James has degrees in history and in law from the University of Chicago and UCLA, and he has held a number of government and think-tank posts in Washington, DC, including at the United States Department of Justice.

Follow him on Twitter @JamesLSwanson

PRAISE FOR OTHER BOOKS BY JAMES L. SWANSON

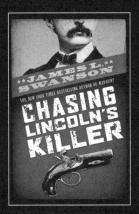

★ "This account of Lincoln's assassination and the 12-day search for his killer reads like a historical thriller...."
—*Publishers Weekly*, **starred review**

★ "The rich details and suspense are ever present.... It is a tale of intrigue and an engrossing mystery."
—*School Library Journal*, **starred review**

"It's history that reads like a tragic thriller."
—*USA Today*

YALSA-ALA Excellence in Young Adult Nonfiction Finalist

★ "Swanson brings the same immediacy and thrillerlike tension he achieved in *Chasing Lincoln's Killer* to this harrowing account of the Kennedy assassination...."
—*Publishers Weekly*, **starred review**

"Swanson charms readers with mesmerizing, little-known facts, making readers the experts and inspiring them to become historians and inquirers."
—*VOYA Magazine*

"... reads like a thriller, with intense pacing and an engaging narrative."
—*School Library Journal*